T0209175

THE
LATE
GREAT
UNITED STATES

What Bible Prophecy Reveals About
America's Last Days

MARK HITCHCOCK

MULTNOMAH
BOOKS

THE LATE GREAT UNITED STATES

Trade Paperback ISBN 978-1-60142-141-8
eBook ISBN 978-1-60142-173-9

Published in the United States by Multnomah, an imprint of the Crown Publishing Group, a division of Penguin Random House LLC, New York.

MULTNOMAH® and its mountain colophon are registered trademarks of Penguin Random House LLC.

The Library of Congress has cataloged the hardcover edition as follows:
Hitchcock, Mark.
    The late great United States : what Bible prophecy reveals about America's last days / Mark Hitchcock.
        p. cm.
    ISBN 978-1-60142-140-1
    1. Bible—Prophecies—United States. 2. United States—-History—Prophecies. 3. Bible—Prophecies—End of the world. 4. End of the world—Biblical teaching. I. Title.
    BS649.U6H59 2008
    220.1′5—dc22
                        2008029232

To my grandfather, Floyd Hitchcock,
whose passion for the Blessed Hope
lives on in me.

TABLE OF CONTENTS

*I think there is an unspoken subtext in our national
political culture right now.
In fact I think it's a subtext to our society.
I think that a lot of people are carrying around in
their heads, unarticulated and even in
some cases unnoticed, a sense that the wheels
are coming off the trolley and the
trolley off the tracks.*

—Peggy Noonan, **Wall Street Journal**

*We are in a country in debt and in decline—
not terminal, not irreversible, but in decline.
Our political system seems incapable
of producing long-range answers
to big problems or big opportunities.*

—Thomas L. Freedman, **New York Times**

*The world has shifted from anti-Americanism
to post-Americanism… The distribution
of power is shifting, moving away from
American dominance."*

—Fareed Zakaria, **Newsweek**

THE QUESTION
EVERYONE'S
ASKING

*I turn back to your prophets in the Old Testament and
the signs foretelling Armageddon, and I find myself wondering if
we are the generation that is going to see that come about.
I don't know if you have noted any of those prophecies lately, but,
believe me, they describe the times we are going through.*
—President Ronald Reagan, 1983

Suppose someone wrote and published the ultimate compendium of music history…but left out any mention of Beethoven, the Beatles, or Garth Brooks.

Or the French produced a video tour of Paris…with nary a glimpse of Notre Dame, the Louvre, or the Eiffel Tower.

Imagine a math textbook containing an entire year's curriculum…never once using or discussing the number one.

When an authoritative resource claims expertise in a particular field of knowledge, we usually expect it to touch on the most prominent subjects within its purview. That's why so many Christians read their Bibles—and biblical prophetic passages in particular—fully confident that it must somehow reveal something about the role of America in the end times. After all, God, who exists in all times, who sees the end of history from the beginning, who indeed sovereignly governs every moment of history—God, who reveals key end-time events in the prophecies of Scripture, can't possibly have omitted from His opus the most powerful, most influential, and by many counts most God-blessed of all nations that have ever risen.

Can He?

By any standard of measurement, America occupies center stage in the world arena. No one disputes the fact that America has a distinctive history, during which it has risen to dominate global affairs. In a quarter of a millennium it has become a nation unlike any other in the history of the world. It has superseded nations with much longer histories. No nation in the history of civilization has exercised greater influence than the United States of America— politically, militarily, economically, culturally, linguistically, and possibly even religiously. As the old saying goes, "When America sneezes, the world catches a cold."

Most of America's ascent has happened in less than one hundred years. America's awe-inspiring rise to superpower status in the twentieth century accelerated to maximum upward velocity in the aftermath of WWII. In an ironic twist, the war's tragic losses delivered America from the poverty of the Great Depression. The United States emerged from WWII better off militarily, politically, and economically than any other nation. Even during the dark days of the cold war, America had the upper hand on the Soviet Union, as was finally proven in the early 1990s when the Soviet Empire unraveled at the seams and America found herself alone at the top.

The Last Superpower

Today, America prevails as the world's lone superpower. The last contender standing. But the "champ's" reign hasn't been the smooth ride that many optimistically envisioned. From the 1950s through the 1980s, many believed that the demise of the Soviet Union would ensure greater global security. Americans envisioned a brave new world free from the tyranny of Soviet communism. Like many dreams, top-dog status hasn't been what most people expected.

We inaugurated the single-superpower era with the first Gulf War in the early 1990s. Operation Desert Storm was a glowing success. The future looked bright. But then the real trouble started. The underground-garage bombing of the World Trade Center on February 26, 1993, was the first assault of Islamic terror on American soil—a dark omen of things to come. Gathering storm clouds loomed closer with the suicide bombing attack on the USS *Cole* in 2000.

Then dawned the darkest day in American history—the devastating attack of 9/11—plunging America headlong into the age of radical Islamic jihad. Radical Islam declared open war on the United States. The stunning attack gripped the nation, a portent of many more to come.

America and its allies invaded Afghanistan in 2001 and launched the Iraq War in 2003—a war that has cost trillions of dollars and thousands of lives.

And most recently? Economic meltdown. Skyrocketing oil prices. The subprime mortgage crisis. The dollar's devaluation to all-time lows. Foreign nations, awash in oil money, buying major U.S. financial institutions. Runaway deficits and an out-of-control federal budget. Smothering debt. The looming threat of radical Islam.

And the worst fear of all—weapons of mass destruction on American soil.

Many are openly saying that anything less than victory in the currently festering conflicts in Iraq and Afghanistan will weaken America's resolve, embolden the jihadists, and force the United States to abdicate its role as world leader and to retreat into isolation.

America's past is glorious and inspiring. Its present is unstable, yet studded with glimmers of cautious optimism.

But what of the future? Is there any sure word?

Americans, the Future, and the Bible

The increasingly frantic tempo of change in modern life fosters a global sense of impending crisis. People everywhere fear that the world is moving rapidly toward some calamity—possibly even a finale. I'm sure you've sometimes wondered what's going to come of all the danger, uncertainty, and instability. How long can the tensions be held in check? How long until the lid blows off? Terrorism—that Bad Thing that used to happen in other places—has rudely intruded into the life of every American. U.S. troops are still in Iraq, still in Afghanistan. Some predict that we might realistically be there for ten years or longer. The epochal conflict with jihadist terror is still in its infancy. What happens when it grows up?

The danger and uncertainty of modern civilization has caused people from all walks of life to ask forward-peering questions as never before. Solemn questions. Searching questions. Questions about the Middle East. Terrorism. Radical Islam. Israel. Global pandemics. Drastic weather changes. Questions about the future.

But the real issue that seems to lurk, thinly veiled, behind all these questions is, Could we be nearing closing time? The Bible is the only authority for addressing this question, and Americans seem to be discussing biblical prophecy more than ever before. Many believe that the Bible contains the answers about earth's final days.

Here's a brief sample of what Americans believe about the book of Revelation and the end times:

- 59 percent believe that the prophecies in Revelation are going to come true.
- Nearly 25 percent believe that the Bible predicted the September 11 attack.
- 35 percent are paying more attention to how news events might relate to the end of the world.

- 17 percent believe the end of the world will happen in their lifetime.[1]

It's clear that most Americans look to the Bible as an accurate guide for the future. It's also evident that the collective American angst about our world's destiny is building. The fuse is lit. There's fire in the hole. Now we're just wondering how long till it's all gonna blow.

As we look into the pages of the Bible, we quickly discover that, as alarming as current events might be, they don't surprise God. The geopolitical situation we see today in the headlines bears a remarkable correspondence to the trend of world events that Bible prophecies foretold millennia ago. As we probe God's Word for clues, we discover the "You Are Here" arrow marking our current position in God's unfolding program, and we notice that some predicted events may occur in our lifetime. Prophecies, which in the past were sometimes carelessly brushed aside as unbelievable, are sparking renewed interest. But perhaps no issue has created more interest than the possible role of America in the end times. This is the question that people everywhere are asking. It's the question that this book will seek to answer.

Inquiring Minds Want to Know

On January 29, 2008, I had the privilege of appearing on a national television program in Texas. After the program, one of the station employees gave me a ride to my next appointment. We talked as we drove, and I learned that he pastors a new church in the area. We discussed various aspects of pastoral ministry and church life, and before long the topic turned to Bible prophecy. As we neared our destination, he said, "There's one question that I have wondered about more than any other issue related to Bible prophecy." I knew what he was going to ask. "Where do you think America fits into biblical prophecy?"

I'm asked this question more—much more—than any other. People ask me this question at churches, at conferences, on radio and television programs. And as I have talked with my friends and colleagues who teach around the United States and around the world, they confirm that the most-asked question in all of Bible prophecy is, What is America's role in the end times? Something inside us wants to know what will ultimately happen to this great land we call the United States of America.

Bible prophecy experts Thomas Ice and Timothy Demy address this nagging question:

> "God bless America!" Is it a prayer, a promise, or a prophecy? We can see and hear the slogan in music, on bumper stickers, in casual conversations, in campaign rhetoric, at historic moments in our nation's life (both joyful and sorrowful), from podiums, in parades, and in a host of other public and religious forums. Will God bless the United States in the future? Is there any sure word of our nation's future in the Bible generally, and the prophetic passages specifically? It's amazing! One of the most frequently asked questions we receive is with regard to the role of the United States in Bible prophecy. Is it fact or fantasy?[2]

When you think about it, our interest in America's role in the end-of-the-world prophecies could be interpreted as a little self-centered. You rarely, if ever, hear someone wondering about the role of New Zealand, Scotland, Australia, Mexico, or Brazil in the end times. Don't the people in these nations matter as much as American citizens? Although our focus on America's destiny might be considered arrogant by non-Americans, it is nevertheless legitimate, because the United States is the most powerful nation in history and the lone surviving superpower in the world today.

Nothing New

The question about America and biblical prophecy goes way back in our history. I don't know who first raised it, but it was certainly in the air in the nineteenth century. In 1859, Frances Rolleston authored a work titled *Notes on the Apocalypse, as Explained by the Hebrew Scriptures: The Place in Prophecy of America and Australia Being Pointed Out*. Rolleston made the case that America was the two-horned beast in Revelation 13.[3] In 1884, Uriah Smith wrote a book titled *The United States in the Light of Prophecy; or, An Exposition of Rev. 13:11–17*. (Authors back then loved long titles.) For Smith it was unthinkable that the United States would not be mentioned in the Bible. He said, "The question naturally arises, what part has the United States to act in these scenes? For it must seem reasonable and probable that a nation which has risen as suddenly as ours, and made such unparalleled progress, must be a subject of divine prophecy."[4] Smith also maintained that America was the beast of Revelation 13:11–17—a view that seems to have prevailed in that day.

Many theories have sprung up since that time. (We'll explore a few of them in depth in the next chapter.) History reveals that people in every generation since the founding of this great nation have wondered about America's future.

We live in interesting times; it's no wonder that the topic attracts ever more fascination.

Is the Whole Thing Going to Fall Apart?

Few may ask this question audibly, but many of us ponder it in the hidden corridors of our minds. Peggy Noonan relates the following poignant story, expressing the foreboding of many Americans today.

A few weeks ago I was reading Christopher Lawford's lovely, candid and affectionate remembrance of growing up in a particular time and place with a particular family, the Kennedys, circa roughly 1950–2000. It's called "Symptoms of Withdrawal." At the end he quotes his Uncle Teddy. Christopher, Ted Kennedy and a few family members had gathered one night and were having a drink in Mr. Lawford's mother's apartment in Manhattan. Teddy was expansive. If he hadn't gone into politics he would have been an opera singer, he told them, and visited small Italian villages and had pasta every day for lunch. "Singing at la Scala in front of three thousand people throwing flowers at you. Then going out for dinner and having more pasta." Everyone was laughing. Then, writes Mr. Lawford, Teddy "took a long, slow gulp of his vodka and tonic, thought for a moment, and changed tack. 'I'm glad I'm not going to be around when you guys are my age.' I asked him why, and he said, 'Because when you guys are my age, the whole thing is going to fall apart.'"

Mr. Lawford continued, "The statement hung there, suspended in the realm of 'maybe we shouldn't go there.' Nobody wanted to touch it. After a few moments of heavy silence, my uncle moved on."[5]

One might be tempted to conclude, "If Ted Kennedy knows that things are going to fall apart, then shouldn't the rest of us?" Maybe we do. Maybe that's why our pop culture has gone apocalyptic. Maybe we all sense that the train has derailed but we just don't want to admit it. We'd rather spend our remaining moments of sweet denial—as the cars plummet from the railroad bridge to the valley floor—enjoying our coffee and Sudoku.

What *does* lie ahead? I'm sure that at one time or another you've wondered where America is headed. You may have asked yourself questions like these:

- Does the Bible have anything to say about America in the last days?
- How could the United States fit into God's prophetic program?
- Will America survive?
- Will the United States be sucked into the Middle East maelstrom?
- Could America's addiction to oil be its undoing?
- Will the United States become part of a North American union with Canada and Mexico?

- Will America be destroyed by a nuclear attack?
- Could America collapse in on itself as a result of moral corruption?
- Is there any hope for America? for the future?

We'll explore these questions and many others in the pages that follow. You may not agree with every conclusion I reach. And that's okay. I welcome your thoughtful interaction as we embark on this exciting and increasingly relevant adventure to discover what the Bible does and doesn't say about America's last days.

2

IS AMERICA
MENTIONED IN
PROPHECY?

*Never before was there a country to which
the people of every land have flocked as they have to this.
America has become the melting pot of the nations,
and as such has exerted, through its principles of government,
a vastly greater political influence upon the world than has ever
been exerted by any other country. Would it then be
unreasonable to expect that inspired prophecy, which has
delineated the course of other and lesser nations,
should have something to say regarding the
career of this great republic?*

—L. A. Smith,
The United States in Prophecy, 1914

*America's geography existed prior to 1492, or Columbus
could not have discovered it! The United States of America is
involved in Bible prophecy, even if many students
have neither discovered nor explored the fact.*

—Douglas B. MacCorkle,
America in History and Bible Prophecy, 1976

God rules over all. He therefore sovereignly controls the birth, lifespan, and demise of every earthly national entity. And while the Bible does not provide information about most nations, it clearly discusses the final destiny of several. At least fifteen nations and regional alliances can read their futures in the pages of Scripture as clearly as if they were reading a history book:

Israel

Jordan (Ammon, Moab, and Edom)

Egypt

Sudan (Cush)

Russia (Rosh)

Iran (Persia)

Iraq (Babylon)

Europe (reunited Roman Empire)

Central Asia (Magog)

Syria

Greece

Saudi Arabia and other Gulf States (Sheba and Dedan)

Libya (Put)

Lebanon (Tyre)

China (kings of the east)

America, like most nations, is not mentioned *specifically by name* anywhere in Scripture. This is obvious, and I know of no prophecy teacher or writer who would deny it. Nevertheless, America is clearly a part of the general framework of prophecy. Numerous passages in the Bible refer to God's final dealings with "all the nations." No one disputes that America is included in these catch-all references. The real question is, Do specific Scripture passages prophesy the role of America in the last days without giving the exact name "America" or "the United States"? Many students of Bible prophecy believe that some do. Join me as we explore and evaluate some of the most common views.

View #1: America Is Babylon the Great

Since the 9/11 terrorist attack, I have heard this question over and over again: is America (or specifically New York City) Babylon the great in Revelation 17–18?

I heard a prophecy teacher on television say that New York City is Babylon and that the fall of the World Trade Center was a fulfillment of Bible prophecy. To support his conclusion he cited Revelation 18:9–11:

> And the kings of the earth, who committed acts of immorality and
> lived sensuously with her, will weep and lament over her when they see
> the smoke of her burning, standing at a distance because of the fear of
> her torment, saying, "Woe, woe, the great city, Babylon, the strong
> city! For in one hour your judgment has come."
>
> And the merchants of the earth weep and mourn over her,
> because no one buys their cargoes any more.

The preacher then pointed to several details the 9/11 attack shares in common with this vivid prophetic description: New York City is the great commercial capital of the world; the whole world could see the smoke of its burning on September 11; the merchants wept over the city; and the World Trade Center was destroyed in "one hour."

This position has many problems, but the most obvious is that Babylon will be destroyed by God at the end of the seven-year Tribulation period, just before the Second Coming of Jesus to defeat the Antichrist's armies at Armageddon. Obviously, 9/11 was not the end of the Tribulation.

Any credible prophecy teacher would agree that the terrorist attack on the World Trade Center does not fulfill Revelation 18–19. But some do maintain that Babylon in Revelation 18–19 is America or New York City.

Making the Case

One of the key individuals who believes that America is Babylon is S. Franklin Logsdon. He finds it inconceivable that God would not mention America in Scripture.

> It would be most unwise to declare that the U.S.A. is not in prophecy, that the Lord did not see these conditions existing here as well as in the other nations of the world.
>
> Actually, it is unthinkable that the God who knows the end from the beginning would pinpoint such small nations as Libya, Egypt, Ethiopia and Syria in the prophetic declaration and completely overlook the wealthiest and most powerful nation on the earth. Too long have we evaded the question.[1]

Logsdon points to sixteen particular parallels between Babylon in Jeremiah 50–51 and modern America. He concludes that America will be destroyed in the last days by a great alliance of nations from the north—probably led by Russia—that possesses devastating weapons and that will strike unexpectedly, suddenly, and decisively.[2]

Jack Van Impe, a popular television prophecy teacher, also affirms that Jeremiah 50–51 and Revelation 18 describe America in the last days. After pointing out several similarities between Babylon and the United States, he concludes, "That, my friends, is a graphic picture of the United States of America."[3]

In another of his books Van Impe says,

> In Revelation, chapter 18, John the Apostle also alludes to this nation—a rich land laden with sins that has glorified herself and lived deliciously.
>
> As I continue to read and study the prophetic writings of Scripture, I become more and more convinced that this is a direct

reference to the United States. The present hedonistic pleasure-craze of our nation will not last forever. America's destruction may come quick as lightning.[4]

America, the Babylon?

R. A. Coombes, in *America, the Babylon: America's Destiny Foretold in Biblical Prophecy*, offers the most extensive, in-depth treatment of the American Babylon view that I've been able to find. He closely examines Jeremiah 50–51; Isaiah 13–14; 18; 21; 24; 47; 48 and then presents thirty-three identifying markers that he says identify the last-days Babylon as the leading city in America—New York City. I'll offer ten of his more interesting claims here:

Future Babylon:

1. Will be "the least of the nations" or last of the superpowers (Jeremiah 50:12).
2. Is where leaders from the nations "stream to" or meet together (Jeremiah 51:44).
3. Is the proverbial world's policeman (Jeremiah 50:23).
4. Is a nation of abundant wealth (Jeremiah 51:13).
5. Is a country of many and varied immigrants (Jeremiah 50:16).
6. Has no fear of invasion (Isaiah 47:5, 8).
7. Is known for disrespecting the elderly (Isaiah 47:6).
8. Is recognized for the "whirring wings" of its air travel and military air power (Isaiah 18:1).
9. Has the ability to "ascend to the heavens" or have a successful space program (similar to the desires of ancient Babylon with its tower of Babel, and perhaps more than just astronomy) (Jeremiah 51:53).
10. Seems to have something like to stealth technology (Isaiah 47:10–13).[5]

From Revelation 17–18, Coombes derives yet another list—in the form of a quiz—of sixty-six points that he claims identify Babylon as New York City. Again, I explain only ten of his more interesting points:

New York City:

1. Is the location of the only world-governing body—that is, the United Nations (Revelation 17:2, 8).
2. Is the city of commodities, trading these items daily:
    Coffee, Sugar and Cocoa Exchange
    New York Cotton Exchange
    New York Mercantile Exchange (NYMEX):
        crude oil, gasoline, natural gas, heating oil, platinum, palladium
    New York Commodities Exchange (COMEX):
        gold, silver, copper
    And also a leader in the marketing of:
        diamonds, precious gems, iron, ivory, marble, spices, cosmetics, legal pharmaceutical drugs, professional services especially related to advertising, media, and the arts; the main import city for fine foreign wines from around the world. (Revelation 18:11–13)
3. Is home to:
    the New York Stock Exchange
    the American Stock Exchange
    the NASDAQ (Revelation 18:15, 19)
4. Is a deep-water port city—one of the world's greatest seaports ever (Revelation 18:17–19).
5. Is the key cultural city of the world (Revelation 18:22).
6. Is the largest consuming city of illicit drugs, especially heavy drugs like heroin and cocaine (Revelation 18:23).
7. Is a city of immigrants and always has been (Revelation 17:15).
8. Is the place for merchandising occultism (Revelation 18:23).
9. Has the largest population of Jews in America, and the United States is home to more Jewish people than anywhere in the world, including Israel (Revelation 18:4; Jeremiah 50:8, 28; 51:6, 45–46).

10. The modern town of Babylon, New York, is on Long Island and over-looks one of the main harbor approaches to New York City; it's within view of the Statue of Liberty. This city received its name because of the large influx of Jewish immigrants settling in the area, because the Jewish population became a reminder of the Jewish exiles in ancient Babylon.[6]

Reasons to Reject This View

While there could be a few interesting parallels between Babylon and New York City, I don't believe this is the best view. I believe Babylon in Revelation 17–18 refers to a literal rebuilt city of Babylon in modern-day Iraq on the Euphrates River, which God will destroy at the end of the Tribulation. I find seven main points in Revelation 17–18 that favor this identification of Babylon.

First, in Revelation the great city that is described as the last-days capital of the Antichrist is specifically called Babylon six times in Revelation (14:8; 16:19; 17:5; 18:2, 10, 21). While it is possible that the name *Babylon* is a code name for Rome, New York, Jerusalem, or some other city, the text contains no indication that the name is meant to be taken figuratively or symbolically. A literal Babylon is the best interpretation.

Second, Babylon is the most-mentioned city in the Bible, other than Jerusalem. Babylon is mentioned about three hundred times in Scripture, and it is consistently pictured as the epitome of evil and rebellion against God. Babylon is Satan's capital city on earth.

1. Babylon is the city where people first began to worship themselves in organized rebellion against God (Genesis 11:1–11).

2. Babylon was the capital city of the first world ruler, Nimrod (Genesis 10:8–10; 11:9).

3. Nebuchadnezzar, king of Babylon, destroyed the city of Jerusalem and the temple in 586 BC.

4. Babylon was the capital city of the first of four Gentile world empires to rule over Jerusalem.

Since Babylon was the capital city of the first world ruler and is pictured as Satan's capital city on earth throughout Scripture, it makes sense that in the end times he will once again raise up this city as the capital of the final world ruler. In Charles H. Dyer's excellent best-selling book, *The Rise of Babylon,* he says, "Throughout history, Babylon has represented the height of rebellion and opposition to God's plans and purposes, so God allows Babylon to continue during the final days. It is almost as though he 'calls her out' for a final duel. But this time, the conflict between God and Babylon ends decisively. The city of Babylon will be destroyed."[7]

Third, the city of Babylon fits the criteria for this city as described in Revelation 17–18. As Robert L. Thomas, a respected New Testament scholar, notes, "Furthermore, Babylon on the Euphrates has a location that fits this description politically, geographically, and in all the qualities of accessibility, commercial facilities, remoteness of interferences of church and state, and yet centrality in regard to the trade of the whole world."[8]

Fourth, the Euphrates River is mentioned by name twice in Revelation. In 9:14, the text states that four fallen angels are being held at the Euphrates awaiting the appointed time for them to lead forth a host of demons to destroy one-third of mankind. In Revelation 16:12, the sixth bowl of judgment is poured out and dries up the Euphrates to prepare the way for the kings of the east. These references point to the fact that something important and evil is occurring at this site. The emphasis on the Euphrates River in Revelation makes sense if the rebuilt city of Babylon on the Euphrates functions as a religious and political center for the Antichrist.

Fifth, Zechariah 5:5–11 records an incredible vision that pertains to the city of Babylon in the last days:

> Then the angel who was talking with me came forward and said, "Look up and see what's coming."
>
> "What is it?" I asked.

He replied, "It is a basket for measuring grain, and it's filled with the sins of everyone throughout the land."

Then the heavy lead cover was lifted off the basket, and there was a woman sitting inside it. The angel said, "The woman's name is Wickedness," and he pushed her back into the basket and closed the heavy lid again.

Then I looked up and saw two women flying toward us, gliding on the wind. They had wings like a stork, and they picked up the basket and flew into the sky.

"Where are they taking the basket?" I asked the angel.

He replied, "To the land of Babylonia, where they will build a temple for the basket. And when the temple is ready, they will set the basket there on its pedestal." (NLT)

The prophet Zechariah, writing in about 520 BC, twenty years after the fall of Babylon to the Medo-Persians, foresees evil returning to its original home in Babylon in the future. In this vision Zechariah sees a woman who is named Wickedness. Then he sees this woman carried away in a basket in the last days to the land of Babylon, where a temple will be built for her.

The parallels between Zechariah 5:5–11 and Revelation 17–18 are striking.

ZECHARIAH 5:5–11	REVELATION 17–18
Woman sitting in a basket	Woman sitting on the beast, seven mountains and many waters (17:3, 9, 15)
Emphasis on commerce (a basket for measuring grain)	Emphasis on commerce (merchant of grain, 18:13)

Woman's name is Wickedness	Woman's name is Babylon the Great, Mother of All Prostitutes and Obscenities in the World (17:5, NLT)
Focus on false worship (a temple is built for the woman)	Focus on false worship (18:1–3)
Woman is taken to Babylon	Woman is called Babylon (17:5)

God's Word teaches that in the end times wickedness will again rear its ugly head in the same place where it began—Babylon. The prostitute of Revelation will fulfill Zechariah 5 as Babylon is established in the last days as the city that embodies evil.

Sixth, since the city of Babylon has, to date, never been destroyed suddenly and completely, as predicted in Isaiah 13 and Jeremiah 50–51, these passages must refer to a future city of Babylon that will be totally destroyed in the Tribulation.

Seventh, Jeremiah 50–51 clearly describes the geographical city of Babylon on the Euphrates. The many parallels between this passage and the future Babylon in Revelation 17–18 indicate that they are both describing the same city:

	JEREMIAH 50–51	REVELATION 17–18
Compared to a golden cup	51:7	17:4; 18:6
Dwelling on many waters	51:13	17:1
Involved with nations	51:7	17:2
Named the same	50:1	18:10
Destroyed suddenly	51:8	18:8
Destroyed by fire	51:30	17:16
Never to be inhabited	50:39	18:21
Punished according to her works	50:29	18:6

Fall illustrated	51:63–64	18:21
God's people flee	51:6, 45	18:4
Heaven to rejoice	51:48	18:20[9]

Therefore, I believe that Babylon in Revelation 17–18 *is not* New York City or America. I believe that the literal city of Babylon will be rebuilt in the last days to serve as the religious and commercial capital for the Antichrist's empire.[10] Wickedness will return to this place for its final stand. Then, at the end of the Tribulation in the seventh bowl of judgment, God will destroy the great city of Babylon with fire (Revelation 17:16; 18:8). Babylon will fall, never to rise again!

The rise of Iraq in recent years on the world political and economic scene, fueled (so to speak) by its huge oil revenues, is not an accident. The ongoing Iraq War is keeping world focus on Iraq. The current rebuilding and rise of Babylon in modern Iraq may be a key part of God's plan for the end times.

View #2: America Is the Unnamed Nation in Isaiah 18

In the quest to find America in the pages of Scripture, another passage that is commonly cited as a reference to the United States is Isaiah 18. This mysterious passage refers to a great nation, not specifically identified by name, whose people are fierce and enterprising. Verses 1–2 issue a warning to this nation:

> Woe to the land shadowing with wings, which is beyond the rivers of Ethiopia: that sendeth ambassadors by the sea, even in vessels of bulrushes upon the waters, saying, Go, ye swift messengers, to a nation scattered and peeled, to a people terrible from their beginning hitherto; a nation meted out and trodden down, whose land the rivers have spoiled! (KJV)

I'm not sure who first related America to Isaiah 18, but I've traced this view back to 1856 and Joseph Augustus Seiss (1823–1904), a popular and influential Lutheran minister from Frederick County, Maryland. His excellent commentary on Revelation has been a standard since it was published.

Seiss, along with many of his British contemporaries, maintained that the "great maritime power" in Isaiah 18 referred to either the United States or England or perhaps both.[11] Seiss notes, "We there read of a great maritime power, spreading wide its wings, existing somewhere in the Far West from Palestine, and which must either be the United States, Great Britain, or perhaps both, as one in religion, language, and laws."[12]

Jack Van Impe supports the view that this is a reference to America:

Isaiah 18:1–2 issues a warning to a nation.… The nation described in this text is in great difficulty with God because the opening word "woe" in the text is judgmental. The nation has the insignia of wings, similar to America's national emblem, the bald eagle. It is a land that is beyond the sea from Israel. This designation of "beyond Ethiopia" eliminates all of the nations of Europe, Asia and Africa. It is a land scattered and peeled, meaning it is stretched out and having a large landmass. It is measured and staked out with counties, cities, and states. It is a land with polluted rivers. Does that not sound unmistakably like our precious America?[13]

The phrase in Isaiah 18:2, "whose land the rivers have spoiled" (KJV), is better translated, "whose land the rivers divide" (NASB). Some see this as a clear reference to America since America is divided east and west, from Canada to the Gulf of Mexico, by the Mississippi and is further divided by the Ohio, Tennessee, Missouri, Arkansas, and Columbia rivers.[14]

In spite of these creative attempts, the biblical evidence *against* identifying America with the nation mentioned in Isaiah 18 is overwhelming. Isaiah 18–20 is a single connected prophecy dealing with the ancient nations of Cush and Egypt, which were united at that time. Ancient Cush included modern-day southern Egypt, Sudan, northern Ethiopia, and Somalia. The phrase "the land shadowing [whirring] with wings" does not refer to the wings of an eagle, but probably to the whirring wings of insects that infested the Nile Valley in that area. The mention of the land being divided by rivers (Isaiah 18:7) is a reference to the various branches of the Nile River that flowed through Cush and Egypt.

In Isaiah 18:1–2, God is warning the Cushites to get in their boats and head back home and not try to form an alliance against the Assyrians. In verse 3, God promised that when it was time for the Assyrians to fall, He Himself would destroy them for all to see: "All you inhabitants of the world and dwellers on earth, as soon as a standard is raised on the mountains, you will see it, and as soon as the trumpet is blown, you will hear it."

If someone wants to find America in Bible prophecy, they will have to look somewhere other than Isaiah 18.

View #3: America Is the Ten Lost Tribes of Israel

British Israelism, which is sometimes also known as Anglo-Israelism, is the belief that many inhabitants of Britain are direct descendants of the ten lost tribes of Israel. Since God looks kindly upon the descendants of Israel, those who claim this relationship often believe that they are favored by God. Most brands of British Israelism correctly maintain that large numbers of the ten northern tribes of Israel were captured and enslaved by the Assyrians when Samaria fell in 722 BC. However, they contend that somehow a number of Israelites, from what they call "the ten lost tribes," eventually made their way to Northern Europe, the British Isles, and with the advent of European colonization even migrated as far as North and South America, Australia, New Zealand, South Africa, and elsewhere around the globe.

In modern times the chief proponent of this view is Herbert W. Armstrong (1892–1986), founder of the Worldwide Church of God. Armstrong says, "The peoples of the United States, the British Commonwealth nations, and the nations of northwestern Europe are, in fact, the peoples of the TEN TRIBES OF THE HOUSE OF ISRAEL."[15] He goes on to note that "the Jewish people are the house of JUDAH.... Here's an astonishing surprise to those who have believed that! The Jews are only a small minority of the Israelites."[16] So, for Armstrong and his followers, Judah is the Jewish people, but the ten lost tribes of the house of Israel are primarily the United States and the British Commonwealth. Armstrong develops his novel interpretation by means of a lengthy, rather complicated method of looking at the meaning of various Hebrew words and taking passage after passage out of context.

One of his main, and very creative, arguments has to do with the northern tribe of Dan. Armstrong argues:

> When Assyria captured Israel, these Danites struck out in their ships and sailed west through the Mediterranean and, as we shall now note, north to Ireland.... Some historians see a connection between those Danites and the Danoi in Greece and the Tuatha De and Tuathe De Danaan of Ireland. *Tuatha De* means "the people of God." The name Dunn in the Irish language, for example, means the same as Dan in the Hebrew: judge. But the northern colony of Danites was taken to Assyria in the captivity, and thence with the rest of the Ten Tribes they traveled from Assyria by the overland route. After leaving Assyrian captivity, they first inhabited the land just west of the Black Sea before migrating northwest. And we find in the directions they journeyed a nation—Denmark today—which is named Danmark by its inhabitants, meaning Dan's borderland or march.[17]

After a great deal of tedious and questionable argumentation, Armstrong finally concludes that America is the northern tribe of Manasseh:

> The truth that we are Manasseh is overwhelming. Manasseh was to separate from Ephraim and become the greatest, wealthiest single nation of earth's history. The United States alone has fulfilled this prophecy.
>
> Manasseh was in fact a *thirteenth* tribe. There were twelve original tribes. Joseph was one of these twelve. But when Joseph divided into two tribes and Manasseh separated into an independent nation, it became a thirteenth tribe. Could it be mere coincidence that it started, as a nation, with *thirteen* colonies?[18]

Reasons to Reject This View

While I could offer many points to refute the idea that America is the lost tribe of Manasseh, here are five key biblical reasons to reject this view.

First, many scholars maintain that when the Jews returned from the seventy-year Babylonian captivity in 538 BC, "exiles from a wide background of tribes, villages, and towns returned."[19] This included people from the ten tribes that British Israelists say lost their identity in 722 BC.

Second, we know that the tribe of Levi, which was one of the ten tribes besides Judah and Benjamin, was not lost. When the remnant returned to the land in 538 BC, the Levites are specifically mentioned in Ezra 1:5. The same was true in the days of Nehemiah in about 440 BC (Nehemiah 7:43). While the tribe of Levi is not mentioned in Revelation 7, the fact remains that Levi did not lose its national identity in 722 BC.

Third, even in the New Testament, people from the ten tribes were still identifiable. For instance, in Luke 2:36, Doctor Luke identifies Anna as a member of the tribe of Asher. If the ten northern tribes lost their identity in the Assyrian captivity in 722 BC, how did Luke know Anna's tribal association in about 5 BC, at the time of Christ's birth?

Fourth, Jeffrey Louie, in his PhD dissertation on the 144,000 in Revelation, writes that the idea of ten lost tribes "can only be described as a presumption based upon ignorance. The concept of a total deportation is not a viable position."[20] Louie notes from 2 Chronicles 30 that many from the Northern Kingdom (the ten northern tribes) came down to the Southern Kingdom (the two southern tribes) and were preserved. Even though a majority from the Northern Kingdom were taken into captivity by the Assyrians, many from the ten tribes remained in the land of Israel. Louie also documents that those taken into captivity maintained their identity while outside their homeland.[21] Louie further documents that "the Ashkenazim, or mainly the descendants of Judah and Benjamin, and the Sepharadim and Oriental Jews are mainly the descendants of the ten northern tribes." He concludes: "Although the tribal genealogies no longer exist, it is wrong to conclude that the descendants of the northern tribes also no longer exist. The northern heritage exists in the modern Jewish population."[22]

Fifth, the Bible teaches that the descendants of Abraham, Isaac, and Jacob, who are scattered all over the earth, will be regathered to their ancient homeland in the end times. The scattering or Diaspora of the Jews began over nineteen hundred years ago, but the regathering has begun in the last century.

Moreover, in Revelation 7:4–7, we see 144,000 Jewish men singled out for special ministry and protection—12,000 from each of the twelve tribes, including the so-called ten lost tribes. While many have tried to spiritualize this prophecy and make it a reference to the church, the clear meaning in its context is that these are literally twelve tribal bloodlines of Israel.[23] The presence of these end-time Jewish witnesses from the twelve tribes means that the ten northern tribes must not have been lost. Many of them have been dispersed, but not lost. God knows where every man, woman, and child of them is located. Those who doubt that God will literally appoint 144,000

Jewish males during the end times are lacking a biblical view of God. Even though tribal identities may be forgotten by mankind, God has never lost track of them—who or where they are. Apologist Norman Geisler rightly notes that the view that the ten northern tribes are lost "is an insult to the omniscience of God. Certainly He who names and numbers the stars (Isaiah 40:26) and will reconstruct the dispersed particles of our decayed bodies in the resurrection both knows who those lost tribes are and how to regather them."[24] And in our own time we are witnessing the initial stages of the final regathering of the Jewish people to their ancient homeland. It has been happening right before our eyes in the modern State of Israel, which was reestablished in 1948.

These ten tribes are not, nor have they ever been, lost. And they are not in any way related to the United States. The United States is not the ten lost tribes of Israel, nor the tribe of Manasseh. Israel is still Israel and will fulfill its central role in the events of the end times, just as the Bible predicts. But more about that later.

View #4: America Is "the Young Lions of Tarshish" in Ezekiel 38

Another Scripture passage that has often been cited as a reference to the United States is Ezekiel 38:13. This verse is found within the greater context of Ezekiel 38–39—one of the most incredible prophecies in the Bible. In order for us to understand 38:13, we must understand a little background from the overall setting of chapters 38–39.

These two chapters, written over twenty-five hundred years ago, predict a last-days invasion of the land of Israel by a massive attack force, led by a man called Gog, who will be the final ruler of Russia or "Rosh." Ezekiel 38:1–6 provides a compelling list of the specific nations that will invade Israel in the end times.

Russia's Allies in the Battle of Gog and Magog

ANCIENT NATION	MODERN NATION
Magog (ancient Scythians)	Central Asia (Kazakhstan, Tajikistan, Turkmenistan, Kyrgyzstan and Uzbekistan)
Meshech	Turkey
Tubal	Turkey
Persia	Iran
Ethiopia (Cush)	Sudan
Libya (Put)	Libya
Gomer	Turkey
Beth-togarmah[25]	Turkey

Many people thought that when the Soviet Union came tumbling down on December 26, 1991, Russia was finished—a modern-day Humpty Dumpty. The mighty Russian bear was believed to have gone into permanent hibernation. However, the Bible predicts that a great northern nation named Rosh with many allies will invade Israel in the end times. When we track this great nation, the tracks lead right into the land of Israel.

When Russia and its allies come sweeping into Israel, God will wipe them off the face of the earth. Ezekiel 38:18–22 describes the fearsome wrath of God against Gog:

"It will come about on that day, when Gog comes against the land of Israel," declares the Lord GOD, "that My fury will mount up in My anger. In My zeal and in My blazing wrath I declare that on that day there will surely be a great earthquake in the land of Israel. The fish of the sea, the birds of the heavens, the beasts of the field, all the creeping things that creep on the earth, and all the men who are on the face of the earth will shake at My presence; the mountains also will be thrown down, the steep pathways will collapse and every wall will fall to the ground. I will call for a sword against him on all My mountains," declares the Lord GOD. "Every man's sword will be against his brother. With pestilence and with blood I will enter into judgment with him; and I will rain on him and on his troops, and on the many peoples who are with him, a torrential rain, with hailstones, fire and brimstone."

God will utterly destroy Gog and his allies by earthquake, infighting among the troops, pestilence (disease), and fire from heaven.

What Does This Have to Do with America?

You might be wondering at this point why we seem to be talking about so many nations other than America. Let me show you the connection that many prophecy scholars see.

Ezekiel 38:13 says that when Russia and its last-days allies descend upon the land of Israel, a small group of nations will lamely protest the invasion. "Sheba and Dedan and the merchants of Tarshish with all its villages will say to you, 'Have you come to capture spoil? Have you assembled your company to seize plunder, to carry away silver and gold, to take away cattle and goods, to capture great spoil?'" These nations won't favor Russia's aggressive presence in the Middle East.

The specific nations that question Gog's actions are identified as "Sheba and Dedan and the merchants of Tarshish." Sheba and Dedan are not difficult to identify; they were ancient names for the lands we know today as Saudi Arabia, Yemen, Oman, and the Gulf States.

Tarshish, on the other hand, is not so simple to identify. At least three locations have been known as "Tarshish" in history. The first was on the east coast of Africa, but the exact location is not known.[26] The second was in England. The third was ancient *Tartessus* in present-day Spain. The weight of authority seems to favor this third site as the biblical Tarshish—a view supported by both Brown-Driver-Briggs and the Hebrew scholar Gesenius.

Tarshish was a wealthy, flourishing colony of the Phoenicians located in modern Spain that exported silver, iron, tin, and lead (Jeremiah 10:9; Ezekiel 27:12, 25). But note that Ezekiel refers not just to Tarshish but to "the merchants of Tarshish with all its villages" (NASB), or "the merchants of Tarshish and all her villages" (NIV). The better translation is probably "Tarshish, with all the young lions thereof" (KJV). The NIV cites "her strong lions" as an alternate reading.

The term "young lions" is often used in Scripture to refer to energetic rulers. Therefore, the young lions who act in concert with Tarshish to verbally oppose Gog's invasion could be strong military and political leaders. Another possibility is that "all the young lions" or "all its villages" refers to the nations that have come out of Tarshish.[27]

Where was Tarshish in Ezekiel's day? It was in the farthest west regions of the known world, in Spain. When God commanded Jonah to go preach to Nineveh (about five hundred miles northeast of Israel), Jonah headed to Tarshish or Spain, which was as far in the other direction as he could go (Jonah 1:1–3).

Tarshish, or modern Spain, could be used by Ezekiel to represent the collective nations of Western Europe who will join Saudi Arabia in denouncing Russia's invasion. Scripture associates Tarshish with the West. For example, "The western kings of Tarshish and other distant lands will bring him tribute" (Psalm 72:10, NLT). The young lions of Tarshish could be a reference to the colonies that emerged from Europe, including the United States. If this is true, then Ezekiel's young lions of Tarshish describes the last-days United

States joining with its European and Saudi–Gulf State allies to lodge a formal protest against the Russian-Islamic aggressors.

If, on the other hand, biblical Tarshish was in England, then the "young lions thereof" could refer to "the United States, Canada, Australia, New Zealand, and other present-day western democracies"[28]—also a clear biblical reference to the role of America in the end times.

Support for This View

Several well-known prophecy teachers favor this view. Ed Hindson says, "As a nation of European transplants, the United States could possibly qualify as the 'young lions' of Tarshish (Ezekiel 38:13, KJV)."[29]

Jack Van Impe believes that America is included in the young lions of Tarshish:

It's true that America is not mentioned in the Bible by name. However, it is written that "all nations" will suffer judgment in the days before the return of our Lord Jesus Christ (Micah 5:15; Ezekiel 39:21). Ezekiel 38:13 does single out Tarshish and all her "young lions," a group of nations that pays a heavy price for coming to the defense of Israel when it is invaded by Russia and a coalition of other nations. The name Tarshish is found twenty times in the Bible and always refers to the land farthest west of Israel. The text refers to the eleven merchants of Tarshish, and explains that these people trade goods around the world. Specifically, I believe Tarshish refers to Britain, and all her "young lions" refers to the English-speaking world—including the United States.[30]

David Allen Lewis also supports this view:

Conservative scholars who interpret the Ezekiel passage literally have tended to identify Tarshish as Great Britain. The young lions thereof would be the English-speaking nations of the world, such as the U.S. and Canada.... This leads us to the exciting conclusion—that this is the one prophecy of the Bible that can be identified with the U.S.... So the young lions of Tarshish would definitely refer to the North American colonies as well as the European colonies, and hence bring the U.S. into this prophecy as one of the nations who will strongly protest the Russian invasion of Israel in the last days.[31]

While I *do not* believe that the young lions of Tarshish refer to the United States, I believe that, of all the specific passages in the Bible that *could* refer to the United States, this is by far the best one. If Tarshish in Ezekiel 38 refers to England, then the case becomes much stronger. But this lone reference seems too tenuous to bring me fully on board with this view.

The Current Alignment of Nations

Whether you take these young lions to refer to the United States or just as a reference to the Western powers of the last days, the scenario presented in Ezekiel 38 fits the present world political situation precisely. Russia continues to build alliances with Middle Eastern nations, especially Iran. The Islamic nations of central Asia (Magog) have developing ties with Iran, Russia, and Turkey. The hatred of the Middle East Muslim nations for Israel continues to fester and boil. It's not too difficult to imagine the nations mentioned in Ezekiel 38:1–6 coming together under Russian leadership to mount a furious attack against Israel.

But who are the Middle East nations that consistently side with the West against the radical Islamic elements in that region? The obvious answer is Saudi Arabia and the other more moderate Gulf States—that is, ancient Sheba and Dedan. The United States and NATO have used bases in these areas to launch strikes against Iraq and to monitor the entire Persian Gulf area. The exact alignment of nations predicted in Ezekiel 38 was clearly in place in the Gulf War in the early 1990s and continues today. The United States, Western Europe, Saudi Arabia, and Kuwait were allied against Iraq while Russia, Iran, Sudan, Libya, and most of the other nations of the Middle East and Persian Gulf were aligned with Iraq, or at least against America. What we see today strikingly foreshadows the biblical prophecy in Ezekiel.

Conclusion

Having examined all the key passages in the Bible that students of Bible prophecy believe could refer to the United States, I conclude that the role of the United States in the end times *is not* specifically discussed in the Bible. This is actually quite remarkable when you think about it. If we are living in the latter years of this age, wouldn't it be important to identify the role of the most powerful, influential nation in the history of the world that also happens to be Israel's principal ally? Over the years, prophecy scholars have struggled to answer this question.

Why is the United States absent? Did God simply choose not to mention America in spite of its immense influence? Or is it missing for some more significant reason? Will the United States suffer some great military defeat? Will our economy implode?

Inquiring minds want to know.

I believe that Scripture offers some important clues about the alignment of nations in the end times that may shed light on America's future.

---- **3** ----

THE LATE
ONCE-GREAT
UNITED STATES

The average age of the world's greatest civilizations
from the beginning of history, has been about two hundred years.
During those two hundred years, these nations always
progressed through the following sequence:
From bondage to spiritual faith;
From spiritual faith to great courage;
From courage to liberty;
From liberty to abundance;
From abundance to complacency;
From complacency to apathy;
From apathy to dependence;
From dependence back into bondage.
—Commonly attributed to Alexander Fraser Tytler

What is the place of America in end-time prophecy? Can we know? Are there any clues?

Does the Bible say anything about the future of the United States? Many are coming to the conclusion that we can know something about America's future. Herman Hoyt, a well-known Bible teacher, writes: "Do the prophetic Scriptures have anything to say about the United States as a world power at the time of the end? To this question the answer must be given in the affirmative. The Scriptures do have something to say, and the picture that is drawn is not bright."[1]

Bible readers must understand that the ancient prophets were primarily concerned with the land of Israel and its immediate neighbors. However, some nations distant from Israel are mentioned in end-time prophecy. Russia (Rosh) is mentioned in Ezekiel 38 as coming from the far north of Israel, and the kings of the east in Revelation 16:12 may include nations as far away as China. The Bible could have easily mentioned America as a great power from the far west. But it's silent. And the silence is significant.

The biblical silence makes it impossible to give any detailed answer to the question of America's role in the end times. However, an examination of the biblical scenario, after the Rapture of the church to heaven, does yield some fascinating clues that I believe shed light on America's last days.

The World Situation at the End Times

To help us find our biblical bearings, let's briefly look at some key end-time markers that help us get a handle on our world's direction. The Bible provides a basic outline of major future events and phases: (1) the Rapture of the church to heaven, (2) a period of further preparation, (3) the signing of a peace treaty that begins the seven-year Tribulation period, and (4) the rise of the Antichrist, who will declare himself world ruler and break the peace treaty with Israel, thereby plunging the world into the Great Tribulation. This ushers in the terrible judgments of the last three and a half years of the end times. Let's consider these events and phases in a little more depth.

1. *The Rapture.* According to the Bible, the next event on God's prophetic calendar is the Rapture of the church. It's an event that could occur at any time and will happen in the time it takes to blink your eye. At the Rapture, the Lord will come in the air and resurrect the bodies of deceased believers,

immediately transporting all living believers into His presence. We'll discuss this amazing future event in more detail in chapter 8.

2. *Time of Further Preparation.* Immediately after the Rapture will be a period of further preparation. It's important to remember that the Rapture doesn't begin the seven-year Tribulation. Between the Rapture and the beginning of the Tribulation will fall a time period that could be days, weeks, months, or possibly even years. An interval of a few months makes the most sense to me. During this time of preparation, a group of ten world leaders will consolidate the power of the West and will emerge on the world stage. This ruling group, committee, or oligarchy will unite the European and Mediterranean countries into a new revived and powerful Western coalition like the Roman Empire. This is the iron fist that will stop the chaos after the Rapture. What we see today in the European Union could be the initial stages of the coming coalition.

3. *The Peace Treaty.* At the conclusion of this period of preparation, a powerful ruler will arise (Daniel 9:26) who will be elected to head the Group of Ten. This charismatic, brilliant leader will launch his career by making a seven-year covenant with Israel (Daniel 9:27). This treaty will introduce a season of protection and peace for Israel, initiated by the leader who will later declare himself world ruler. This "little horn" of Daniel 7:8 will later be revealed as the coming world dictator, who will secure for himself the power consolidated by the Group of Ten. The peace treaty marks the beginning of what is generally described as the seven-year Tribulation.

These predictions fit well with what we see today. People throughout our world are yearning for peace—almost desperately—especially in the Middle East. Historically, America has been the key mediator in the Middle East peace negotiations. But that's changing. The heralded "Roadmap to Peace" was laid out in 2003 by a powerful quartet: the United States, the European Union, the United Nations, and Russia. While the United States still maintains an important Middle East presence, the EU is rising to play a greater and greater role. The EU has a new office of Middle East peace envoy to bring peace to the war-torn region.

It's easy to see how America could passively resign itself from its role as world policeman after the Iraq War ends. Americans are already suffering serious fatigue from this war, and it seems highly probable that the United States will adopt an isolationist posture when the missions in Iraq and Afghanistan are over. This will pave the way for Europe to move in and fill the diplomatic vacuum—just as one would expect in light of the biblical prophecies that the end-time Roman Empire will become the great world power of the end times—and will forge the Middle East peace predicted in Daniel 9:27. The peace process for Israel is exactly following the pattern the Bible predicted more than twenty-five hundred years ago.

4. *The World Dictator.* The world leader who heads the Group of Ten (described as the head of a revived Roman Empire) will break his covenant with Israel after three and a half years (Daniel 9:27). He will declare himself world dictator and proclaim himself god. These earthshaking events will usher in the time that Jesus called the Great Tribulation (the final three and a half years of the seven-year Tribulation). Revelation 13:4, which refers to this coming world ruler as "the beast," says that when he takes the reins of power, no one will be able to successfully mount a challenge to his military authority. "And they worshiped the beast, saying, 'Who is like the beast, and who is able to wage war with him?'" By the midpoint of the Tribulation, his military power will be unrivaled.

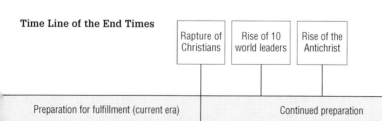

Time Line of the End Times

| Rapture of Christians | Rise of 10 world leaders | Rise of the Antichrist |

| Preparation for fulfillment (current era) | Continued preparation |

No Longer a Superpower

As much as we desire to know about America's future, we face the frustration that America is not clearly, specifically mentioned in Bible prophecy. As noted prophecy expert Tim LaHaye observes, "One of the hardest things for American prophecy students to accept is that the United States is not clearly mentioned in Bible prophecy, yet our nation is the only superpower in the world today."[2] While it would be nice if Scripture clearly laid out the role of the United States in the last days, the silence of Scripture on this subject may tell us more than we realize. The sounds of silence may provide us with the main clue concerning last-days America.

What seems perfectly clear from the biblical scenario of the end times, especially Revelation 13, is that by the middle of the Tribulation, the world dictator will lead the only superpower in the world. Even if the United States has an alliance with the revived Roman Empire, it appears that something will have happened to the United States' role as the world's policeman. It will simply drop out as a superpower.

America will no longer be the leader of nations, but a follower. The end-time events do not include America as the great international heavyweight it is at the beginning of the twenty-first century. As Herman Hoyt notes, "Since the Scriptures are quite as eloquent in their silence as in their statement, it would be well to conclude that absence of any clear reference to the United

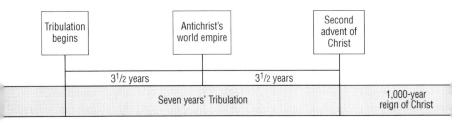

States in the end times as a world power is doubtless to be traced to the fact that it is no longer a world power."[3]

The scriptural silence concerning America seems to indicate that, by the time the Tribulation period arrives, America will no longer be a major influence in the world. John Walvoord, one of the foremost experts in Bible prophecy, agrees with this conclusion: "Although conclusions concerning the role of America in prophecy in the end time are necessarily tentative, the scriptural evidence is sufficient to conclude that America in that day will not be a major power and apparently does not figure largely in either the political, economic, or religious aspects of the world."[4]

Popular theologian Charles Ryrie concurs:

The Bible has made crystal clear the destiny of many nations. Babylon, Persia, Greece, Rome, Egypt, Russia, and Israel.... But not so with the United States....

When Ezekiel described the future Russian invasion he used the phrase "remote parts of the north" (38:15). Surely some prophet would have predicted something about those countries or peoples in the remote parts of the West if God had intended a major end-time role for them in the Western Hemisphere.

The fact is that no one did.

Ryrie concludes that either the United States will be subordinated to a minor role or be neutralized by nuclear fallout or a natural catastrophe before the end times.[5]

To be sure, I don't want to see the United States decline. I love this country. But I agree with Ryrie. It does seem unlikely the United States will play a key role in the end times. But what could reduce America to a subordinate role as ten Western leaders consolidate the West's political, economic, and military power? What kind of event could bring America to its knees? While we cannot speak with certainty at this point—since the Bible doesn't tell us—we can make some educated guesses. Several possibilities fit the current world situation. They could occur alone…or in a fatal combination. We'll examine these, first by looking at a problem of which every American is painfully aware, a problem that could bring the mighty superpower to its knees.

4

OIL:
AMERICA'S
ACHILLES HEEL

*The United States consumes more gasoline
than the next twenty countries combined.*
—Lester Brown, Earth Policy Institute

The U.S. consumes 7.6 billion barrels of oil each year.
—*Time* Magazine

Oil today is forty times its price in 1970.
—Scott Burns, MSN's MoneyCentral

I first used the following illustration in my book, *Armageddon, Oil and Terror* (Tyndale, 2007). Imagine the day the price of oil doubles…or triples. Or is unavailable. The breaking news of the hour may be a hurricane or earthquake that has wiped out ports and refineries, a terrorist attack on the energy infrastructure in Saudi Arabia, an eruption of the Middle East crisis that threatens to spread into a regional conflict, the sinking of supertankers in the Strait of Hormuz, or a nuclear interchange in the Middle East. As with the events of 9/11 or news of any disaster, people around the world will watch in shock. Few who watch the initial news reports will foresee how one or two localized catastrophes will change the world forever. The real shock will come later, when the domino called "the oil break point" tips and falls.

Picture the scenario: Most people rush to the closest gas station only to find handwritten Sold Out signs on the pumps. Blocks-long lines of cars and trucks lead to the dwindling few with any supplies left. In the panic, many people fill up while their tanks are only half full. Gas containers disappear from stores. People begin to hoard, which makes matters worse. Countries also begin to hoard. One by one, the industrial powers of the world announce the need to build massive strategic petroleum reserves. New restrictions and taxes on energy immediately become every government's priority.

A black market in heating oil, gas, and diesel fuel springs up overnight. People focus on their worries about the coming winter. How will they heat their homes? How can they afford the higher utility bills? Will their savings last that long?

Commuters depending on cars can't get to work. Airlines cancel flights and apply for government subsidies. Truckers, who serve as the vital lifeline from warehouses to consumers, refuse to load freight until they have guarantees of stable fuel prices. The streets and highways fall silent. Docks are filled with unmovable freight as the transportation chain breaks down. Ships form long lines at sea as they wait to offload their cargo at their appointed ports.

Those who are able to get to work face looming uncertainties for continued employment. Those businesses and factories that depend on transportation for timely or last-minute supplies now need to slow production or even shut down completely. Even assembly lines with a large supply of parts can't ship their finished products to customers. Stores close when inventories are wiped out, unable to be replenished. The resulting civil unrest forces governments to enact martial law and call out the military to enforce it.

Yes, these scenes come from my imagination. It's difficult to know just how the oil break point would affect you, your family, your employer, and your community. But it's too late to pretend it can't happen.

The headlines reveal the painful truth:

- "Breaking Point: For many Americans, stratospheric oil prices are proving to be the last straw" (*Businessweek,* June 9, 2008)
- "Oil exports are unable to keep up with demand" (*Wall Street Journal,* May 29, 2008)
- "Tapped Out: World oil demand is surging as supplies approach their limits" (*National Geographic,* June 2008)
- "No end seen in reliance on fossil fuel" (Associated Press, June 26, 2008)
- "We Were Warned: Out of Gas" (CNN, June 21, 2008)

If the supply of oil—or the energy infrastructure that refines and distributes oil—hits the breaking point, the economy of the United States and other industrial giants will destabilize. Disruption in the price and availability of oil will destroy third world countries already struggling for survival. The break point will come when demand suddenly exceeds supply. Oil futures on the commodity markets will spike. Nations will rush to hoard more strategic reserves. The high cost of petroleum products alone will cause the wheels of Western economic growth to grind to a halt. On that day the world will be changed forever.[1]

Running on Empty

To power and fuel our modern lifestyle, the world consumes about 86 million barrels of oil *every single day.* This translates into a staggering one thousand barrels per second. To help us grasp the enormity of this, picture an Olympic-size swimming pool. We drain one every fifteen seconds. Every day we empty about fifty-five hundred such swimming pools. And demand continues to rise each year.[2] This means one thing for all Americans: higher prices in almost every expense category.

On January 2, 2008, oil momentarily topped the $100-a-barrel mark for the first time. February 18 was the day the markets first closed with the price over $100 a barrel. On March 12 it climbed past the $110 mark. On April 16, another "ceiling" burst—the $115 barrier. And as I send this manuscript for publication, we had passed into the $140-plus range. But these new record oil prices won't be the last. Concern—even fear—is growing that the supply and price of oil could reach a break point that could send the U.S. economy into full cardiac arrest.

One way to put the oil crisis in perspective is to consider that the value of the entire United States is 400 billion barrels of oil. That's right—you could buy the entire country for 400 billion barrels of oil. The collective net worth of this country is $56 trillion. When you divide that number by $140 for a barrel of oil, you get 400 billion barrels. That's a little less than the proven oil reserves of just two Middle East countries: Saudi Arabia (264 billion barrels) and Iran (139 billion barrels).[3]

With the razor thin margin between supply and demand, a single catastrophe can have devastating economic consequences for consumers. As I wrote in my previous book *Armageddon, Oil and Terror,* think back to when Hurricane Katrina hit the coast. Refineries stopped. Ports were blocked. The price of gas soared. Oil companies reported record profits.

These recent events emphasize a truth most Americans would rather ignore: we have vulnerabilities. One of the greatest is our dependence on foreign oil. The economic concrete of our lives is actually wet cement. The wheels of transportation that make capitalism possible depend on gas, diesel, and high-octane jet fuel. If the wheels stop, our economy will shatter. This slender supply line stretches around the globe to Saudi Arabia, Iraq, Iran, and the Middle East.

New industrial nations are maturing explosively, complete with ravenous energy appetites. Rocketing economic growth in China and throughout Asia creates an unyielding demand for ever-increasing amounts of oil. Scant worldwide supplies barely meet demand. This resulting conflict of economic engines cries out for more oil when supplies are nearing the breaking point. In this decade, economic growth alone will cause an oil break point.

In 2001, Osama Bin Laden plotted to overthrow the monarchy in Saudi Arabia so he could take control of the oil the West so desperately relies on. Then he could have demanded any price. Demanded anything. The plan resulted in the failed 2006 terrorist attack on the heart of the Saudi Arabian oil and gas industry—the Abqaiq processing facility—for which Al Qaeda claimed responsibility. The *New York Times* called it the first attack on Saudi Arabia's oil infrastructure. A day later the story disappeared from the news.

Do these events serve as a dashboard warning indicator for the speeding Western juggernaut? *Check Engine! Brake Failure! Dangerously Low Oil!* Do they foreshadow our near future? What will happen when Islamic terrorists, eager to destroy the U.S. economy, are willing to ignite chaos in the Middle East to bring down the Great Satan of the West? Is it possible to protect every wellhead, pipeline, processing facility, and tanker? Who will stop the sabotage, the trucks laden with explosives, the handheld rockets?

Check Oil

In early 1999, the price of oil was $10 a barrel. Those were the good ol' days. Consider what's happened in the decade since.

- Since 1999 annual oil revenues for OPEC nations have more than quadrupled, to an estimated $670 billion in 2007.
- The price of a barrel of oil has gone from $10 to over $140 at the time of this writing.
- China's oil use has almost doubled to about 7.5 million barrels a day in 2007. That's a full 100 percent increase in just eight years!
- World oil consumption was up 13 percent from 1999 to 2007. America's oil use increased 7 percent during that time.[4]

According to the Department of Energy, the United States currently consumes more than 20 million barrels of oil a day, importing about 60 percent of it, although some put the number at closer to 70 percent. Of the oil that's imported, 70 percent of it is consumed by transportation. Americans spend in excess of $20 billion each year on oil from the Middle East. Twenty years from now, U.S. consumption will rise to almost 30 million barrels of oil a day, at least 70 percent of it imported. This heavy reliance on foreign oil makes America increasingly dependent on some of the least stable countries in the world, which are thousands of miles away. The United States currently gets about 45 percent of its oil from the Middle East and North Africa, regions that hold more than two-thirds of the oil reserves worldwide. The United States consumes three times more oil than it produces, and it consumes most of the oil produced by neighbors Canada and Mexico as well. However, even these resources are not enough. In order to fuel its oil addiction, the United States must import from unstable or state-owned oil companies in Saudi Arabia, Venezuela, and Nigeria, among others. As world oil demand rises, we all will be more dependent on the most oil-rich countries.

It doesn't take much of a disruption in Africa or the Middle East to stifle and stunt supply and dramatically increase the price of oil. For example, according to the Energy Policy Research Foundation, "War, civil strife and nationalization have depressed production in Iraq, Nigeria, Iran, Venezuela and elsewhere. Total global capacity might be 4.5 mb/d [million barrels per day] higher without these setbacks."[5] Nigeria is a major supplier to the United States, and its production has been cut because of attempts by rebels to cripple its oil infrastructure. The U.S. economy is dependent on the steady supply of affordable gasoline, and this supply is becoming less and less dependable and stable. The U.S. economy, in large part, is now in the hands of oil-rich third-world nations, many of which are corrupt, volatile, and unpredictable.

Frederick W. Smith, a former marine, Vietnam vet, and FedEx founder, sounds a sober warning about America's energy crisis. When his company ran simulations, he says that they found a dramatic result: very small reductions in supply have enormous implications for our economy and our security as a nation.[6] This is one reason Smith wants to help craft a sensible energy policy for America. As he points out, our country's dependence on foreign oil is only slightly less a risk factor than terrorism and weapons of mass destruction.[7]

Smith adds:

> The proximate cause of World War II was the U.S. oil embargo against Japan, when we were an oil-exporting nation.... The first gulf war was caused totally by oil—it was Saddam Hussein's insistence that he own certain oilfields that led to his invasion of Kuwait and our ouster of his forces there. The subsequent presence of the United States in the Middle East was in large measure driven by the protection of the oil trade.[8]

Smith's next statement is shocking: "A lot of analysts think that as much as 40 percent of the entire U.S. military budget can be attributed to protecting the oil trade."[9] This highlights a sobering reality: oil is a fundamental security issue in our nation.

Oil Prophets

For some time now experts have been predicting that the world will soon reach its peak in oil production. The so-called peak will be a key line of demarcation for the world and its energy future. When the peak is reached, today's transient shortages and high prices will become a permanent way of life. And some believe the oil crest may be right around the corner.

The simple problem is that worldwide demand for oil is rising rapidly and oil production can't keep up. The IEA (International Energy Agency) projects at least a 50 percent increase in the demand for oil by the year 2030. *USA Today* reports,

> There's no question that demand is rising. Last year, global oil con-
> sumption jumped 3.5 percent, or 2.8 million barrels a day. The U.S.
> Energy Information Administration projects [worldwide] demand
> rising from the current 84 million barrels a day to 103 million barrels
> by 2015. If China and India—where cars and factories are proliferat-
> ing madly—start consuming oil at just one-half of current U.S. per-
> capita levels, global demand would jump 96 percent, according to
> Nur.... Such forecasts put the doom in doomsday.[10]

The world's top oil producers appear to be in trouble. They have been unable to keep up with the thirsty world markets. According to the *Wall Street Journal*, "net oil exports from the world's top 15 exporters—nearly half of all the world's supply—fell almost one million barrels a day in 2007. This means that petroleum exports from the world's top oil producers fell 2.5 percent in 2007. The Middle East's six largest oil exporters reduced their output by 544,000 barrels a day in 2007. Adam Robinson, an oil analyst at Lehman Brothers in New York says, 'The sense in the market is that peak oil is here and that things will only get worse.'"[11]

It doesn't take an economist to recognize that slowing or declining world production coupled with growing demand will drive prices ever higher. A ninety-one-page study prepared in February 2005 for the U.S. Energy Department concluded: "The world is fast approaching the inevitable peaking of conventional world oil production...[a problem] unlike any yet faced by modern industrial society."

Lester Brown, from the Earth Policy Institute, maintains that world oil production could be peaking. Others believe that the peak is already here.

A reasonable date for the oil peak is in the 2010–2015 range. Brown points out that different nations will reach this point at different times:

> The pre-peak countries are dominated by Russia, now the world's leading oil producer, having eclipsed Saudi Arabia in 2006. Two other countries with substantial potential for increasing output are Canada, largely because of its tar sands, and Kazakhstan, which is developing the Kashagan oil field in the Caspian Sea, the only large find in recent decades. Other pre-peak countries include Algeria, Angola, Brazil, Nigeria, Qatar, and the United Arab Emirates.
>
> Among the countries where production may be peaking are Saudi Arabia, Mexico, and China. The big question is Saudi Arabia. Saudi officials claim they can produce far more oil, but the giant Ghawar oil field—the world's largest by far and the one that has supplied half of Saudi oil output for decades—is 56 years old and in its declining years. Saudi oil production data for the first eight months of 2007 show output of 8.62 mb/d [million barrels per day], a drop of 6 percent from the 9.15 mb/d of 2006. If Saudi Arabia cannot restore growth in its oil production, then peak oil is on our doorstep.[12]

The United States, where 88 percent of our workforce commutes every day by car, is much more vulnerable to skyrocketing gasoline prices than many other nations that have efficient, widespread public transportation.[13] Gas prices of four dollars a gallon mean that the average price to fill up a basic automobile is about seventy dollars and costs about three thousand dollars a year for an average fifteen-thousand-mile-a-year driver.[14] The oil peak is very bad news for the United States.

Of course, when we reach the oil peak, the fall on the other side might be gentle. We can expect a plateau period. But at some point—the oil break point, when worldwide demand consistently exceeds available production—our already fragile economy will begin to hemorrhage. Brown cautions that the "peaking of world oil production will be a seismic event, marking one of the great fault lines in world economic history." He notes that when the availability of oil is reduced, no country will get unless another gets less. Flight fares will go up, the prices of growing and transporting food, and gas prices could cause recession, or worse, a 1930s-like depression.[15]

The Great Depression revisited. That's a pretty ominous outlook. But the words of Kenneth Deffeyes, a Princeton University professor emeritus of geosciences, are outright apocalyptic: "The least-bad scenario is a hard landing, global recession worse than the 1930s. The worst-case borrows from the Four Horsemen of the Apocalypse: war, famine, pestilence and death." As global demand rises, American consumers could easily find themselves in a bidding war with others around the world for scarce oil supplies. That will send prices of gasoline, heating oil, and all petroleum-related products soaring.[16]

Another Web site makes this prediction: "In practical and considerably oversimplified terms, this means that if 2005 was the year of global Peak Oil, worldwide oil production in the year 2030 will be the same as it was in 1980. However, the world's population in 2030 will be both much larger (approximately twice) and much more industrialized (oil-dependent) than it was in 1980. Consequently, worldwide demand for oil will outpace worldwide production of oil by a significant margin. As a result, the price will skyrocket, oil-dependent economies will crumble, and resource wars will explode."[17] As nations scramble to meet their energy needs, violent clashes for the precious black gold will become a certainty. Many believe that the resource wars for the Middle East have already begun.

But is this future avoidable? If so, where will the oil come from? Is there any hope in the foreseeable future?

PROVED OIL RESERVES BY COUNTRY (2006)

RANK	COUNTRY	RESERVES (BILLION BARRELS)
1.	Saudi Arabia	264.3
2.	Canada	178.8
3.	Iran	132.5
4.	Iraq	115.0
5.	Kuwait	101.5
6.	United Arab Emirates	97.8
7.	Venezuela	79.7
8.	Russia	60.0
9.	Libya	39.1
10.	Nigeria	35.9
11.	United States	21.4
12.	China	18.3
13.	Qatar	15.2
14.	Mexico	12.9
15.	Algeria	11.4
16.	Brazil	11.2
17.	Kazakhstan	9.0
18.	Norway	7.7
19.	Azerbaijan	7.0
20.	India	5.8
	Top 20 Countries	1,224.5 (95%)
	Rest of World	68.1 (5%)
	World Total	1,292.6

Source: www.infoplease.com/ipa/A0872964.html

Can Coal and Tar Sands Save Us?

As America searches for a way out of its energy dilemma, two sources are often mentioned—coal and tar sands. There's no doubt about it, America is rich in coal. The United States has the largest recoverable coal deposits in the world, estimated at about 268 billion tons. Coal is mined in twenty-six states, but the king of coal is Wyoming.

In spite of deep concerns about its adverse effects on the environment, demand for the commodity is hot. Six hundred power plants in the United States still burn coal and produce about half of America's electricity. Voracious demand for coal in Asia drove the price up 50 percent in late 2007 and early 2008, surpassing the rise in oil prices. China has about 126 billion tons of recoverable coal deposits, but it's burning them as fast as it can get them out of the ground.[18] This is good news for the United States, because as China uses more coal than it can produce, it will have to turn to the United States for supply. But while our coal deposits may help offset some of our huge trade imbalances with China and other nations, coal won't power our cars and trucks.

What about tar sands? Aren't billions of barrels of oil locked in the rich deposits of Canada? It is true that Canada has rich tar-sands deposits. But John Hess, CEO of Hess Corporation, says their potential impact on the skyrocketing demand for oil is negligible. Canada and Venezuela are the two known, big tar-sands deposits, producing 1.7 million barrels a day (he estimates 4 million barrels a day by 2015). But Hess adds,

> The world is consuming 86 million barrels a day.... We don't just
> need more investment in tar sands; we need a whole new oil province
> every year, a new Azerbaijan or Alaskan North Slope. The recent dis-
> coveries in Brazil's Santos Basin are very exciting, and very promising.
> But you're probably not going to get much new supply from it until

eight or ten years from now, and by then we're going to need a new one at least as big.[19]

Moreover, "wringing oil from the sludge-like tar sands is difficult and costly, and requires enormous quantities of water and natural gas—itself an ever-pricier fuel."[20] Tar sands will clearly help, but they aren't the answer to our problem either. Worldwide demand will continue to outstrip the ability of tar sands to keep up. Hess identifies the core of the problem: "About 50 percent of oil demand is for transportation, and auto ownership in the developing countries is growing swiftly, especially in India and China. Goldman Sachs estimates that by 2050, they could have 1.1 billion cars on the road, up from just 20 million three years ago. That's an overwhelming increase in the need for automotive fuel. Put those two things together—limited supply and increasing demand—and you get high oil prices."[21]

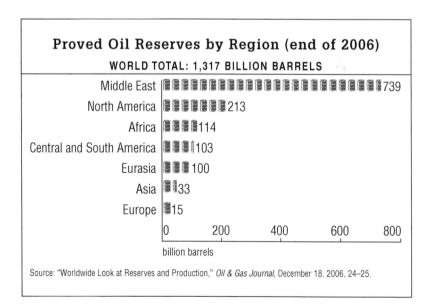

Proved Oil Reserves by Region (end of 2006)
WORLD TOTAL: 1,317 BILLION BARRELS

Region	billion barrels
Middle East	739
North America	213
Africa	114
Central and South America	103
Eurasia	100
Asia	33
Europe	15

Source: "Worldwide Look at Reserves and Production," *Oil & Gas Journal*, December 18, 2006, 24–25.

Hess gives this final warning: "The IEA predicts global demand to average 98.5 million barrels a day by 2015; it's hard to see how we can meet that level of production."[22] The day of reckoning could be only a few years away.

If the United States is going to heal its Achilles heel, it will have to look beyond coal and tar sands. Some believe they have found that answer in biofuels and oil shale. But have they?

Biofuels and Oil Shale Won't Solve the Problem

Many hold out hope that biofuels will save America from the coming oil break point. The primary bio- or agrofuel is ethanol—that is, ethyl alcohol distilled from plant matter. Many maintain that ethanol produced from corn and soybeans is the answer to our foreign oil addiction and that biofuels will have the important side benefit of curbing global warming. With this great optimism, the United States has quintupled its production of ethanol in the past decade. In December 2007, President George W. Bush signed a bipartisan energy bill that dramatically increases support for the biofuel industry by mandating 36 billion gallons of biofuel by 2022. Some consider biofuels to be the new dotcoms, which would make Iowa today's Silicon Valley. Iowa has so many agrofuel distilleries under construction that the state is predicted to become a net importer of corn. The estimated size of the 2010 biofuel market is $100 billion.

Biofuel is a favorite of politicians. They gain popularity and feel they're accomplishing something constructive when they talk about reducing oil dependence, reducing global warming, and satisfying the farm lobby. About 150 ethanol plants currently exist, with the capacity to produce 8.5 billion gallons of fuel each year. Another 61 plants are planned, which will add about 5.1 billion gallons of capacity. Biofuel plants are under construction in New York, Georgia, Oregon, and Texas. However, the rise in corn prices has slowed or halted some of the plants, shaving about 500 million gallons of capacity from the original figure.[23]

The United States is not alone in the biofuel craze. Worldwide investment in biofuels rose from $5 billion in 1995 to $38 billion in 2005. And it's expected to rise to $100 billion by 2010, thanks to a host of big-time investors.

But just as quickly as it has expanded, the ethanol bubble seems to be bursting. This is happening for three principal reasons.

First, biofuels are not reducing the danger of global warming. This has the greenies seeing red. Michael Grunwald, writing for *Time,* calls the biofuel craze "the Clean Energy Myth" and "the Clean Energy Scam."[24] He says, "Several new studies show the biofuel boom is doing exactly the opposite of what its proponents intended: It's dramatically accelerating global warming, imperiling the planet in the name of saving it. Corn ethanol, always environmentally

World Oil Consumption (2007)		
RANK	COUNTRY	AMOUNT (BARRELS PER DAY)
1.	United States	20,730,000
2.	China	6,534,000
3.	Japan	5,578,000
4.	Germany	2,650,000
5.	Russia	2,500,000
6.	India	2,450,000
7.	Canada	2,294,000
8.	South Korea	2,149,000
9.	Brazil	2,100,000
10.	France	1,970,000
	Total	48,955,000

Source: *CIA World Factbook,* June 14, 2007

suspect, turns out to be environmentally disastrous." Grunwald also notes that in Brazilian rain forests, a chunk the size of Rhode Island (750,000 acres) has been cleared just in the last six months of 2007 to make way for ethanol-bound soybean crops to boost the local economy. That's 750,000 deforested acres in six months!

By means of such tragic and expensive trial and error, we're discovering that the only ethanol efficient enough to cut emissions by more than it takes to produce is sugarcane-based ethanol.

Second, the agrofuel boom is causing a dramatic rise in food prices and even shortages in some places. Some have called agrofuels a "crime against humanity," pitting "the 800 million people with cars against the 800 million with hunger problems."[25] Harvests are being reaped for fuel, not food. Corn is the primary feeder stock for U.S. ethanol, which consumed about 20 percent of the corn crop in 2007 and is expected to wolf down 30 percent of the crop in the year ending August 2009.[26] With this soaring demand, corn prices shot up nearly 30 percent in 2008. Prices for meat and pork are also rising as livestock producers are forced to thin their herds and pass on the higher costs of animal feed.[27] The UN World Food Program calls the rise in food prices due to agrofuels a "global emergency." Think about this sobering fact: the corn required to fill an ethanol-fueled SUV would feed one person for 365 days. If the biofuel boom for corn and soybeans continues, food prices could spiral out of control. Grunwald notes, "The lesson behind the math is that on a warming planet, land is an incredibly precious commodity, and every acre used to generate fuel is an acre that can't be used to generate food needed to feed us or the carbon storage needed to save us."[28] The world is already experiencing what some call "agflation" as food prices soar. The world food crisis has begun to boil over in places. Farmers simply can't keep up with rising demand. The world's wheat stocks are at thirty-year lows. While some of this is due to rising fuel costs, drought, and diet changes in Asia, record biofuel production is doing its share of damage in lifting worldwide demand, thus contributing to the world's growing food crisis.[29]

Third, biofuels will hardly make a dent in U.S. oil dependence. Consider this: the United States is the world's number-one producer of corn and soybeans, but even if 100 percent of U.S. corn and soybean production were turned into fuel, it would only offset 20 percent of on-road fuel consumption. The bottom line is that biofuels aren't a real solution for America's growing energy needs for the foreseeable future.

One final alternative that holds some promise for America's energy thirst is oil shale. The United States Geological Survey (USGS) announced in April 2008 that the Bakken shale formation in Montana and western North Dakota may hold as much as 4.3 billion barrels of "undiscovered, technically recoverable oil." The USGS hails the site as the largest "continuous oil accumulation" it has ever assessed. Compare this discovery with the Alberta oil sands, thought to hold about 175 billion to 300 billion barrels of recoverable oil, and Saudi Arabia, which claims upwards of 260 billion. So while 4.3 billion is a significant number and any new discoveries are helpful, Bakken's not in the big leagues. The United States consumes 7.6 billion barrels of oil every year. The oil shale in Montana and North Dakota would only provide enough oil to keep America running for about six months. Moreover, while oil is technically recoverable from these formations, it won't be easy or cheap. The shale is two miles underground.[30] High oil prices and new technology could yield substantial new supplies from the shale. Time will tell. But even if this find is everything experts hope, it will only push the gathering crisis a little further down the road.

"The Answer, My Friend, Is Blowin' in the Wind"

Some are advocating wind power to solve America's energy crisis. T. Boone Pickens, chairman of BP Capital, believes that generating power via renewable sources such as nuclear plants or wind and solar power would allow the United States to shift much of its natural gas resources over to transportation. He maintains that natural gas is the only fuel that can help when it comes to transportation. According to Pickens, shifting to renewable resources for electricity generation and to natural gas for transportation would reduce the need for oil imports by almost 40 percent. Pickens views wind power as the quickest solution but notes that solar could come along to help ease the crunch. He believes that "wind power alone could meet the nation's future electricity power needs in the next 10 years."[31] If he's correct and if America has the vision and will to move in that direction, natural gas could hold at least part of the answer to the coming oil break point for America. But Pickens is realistic when he notes, "You are not going to be able to get away from oil, natural gas and diesel. That is going to be going on for some time. But you can relieve the pressure on those resources."[32] Of course, the problem is that natural gas is also a finite resource, and it too has been steadily escalating in price.

For the foreseeable future, the only measures that appear capable of saving America from itself are meaningful conservation, using wind and solar power for generating electricity, and a corresponding shift to natural gas for transportation needs. Also, some form of viable, affordable hydrogen fuel cell technology for automobiles down the line could help ease America's oil dependence. But so far Americans have not shown much collective will to cut back on gasoline consumption, the shift to renewable sources is slow, and viable hydrogen fuel technology is decades away.

A *Really* Inconvenient Truth

America still clings to its place as the world's lone superpower, but that status could be permanently altered if we are still addicted to imported oil when we reach the break point—when the oil crisis finally peaks and the entire world energy complex scrambles to rebalance itself, stake out energy claims, and adjust to the new situation. Michael Klare, author of *Rising Powers, Shrinking Planet,* calls the redrawing of political and military alliances based on oil reserves the "new international energy order."[33] Nations with substantial oil reserves will enjoy greater and greater international influence. This new order will have dramatic impact on the world's and America's futures, especially as supplies begin to dwindle and demand soars. According to some experts, we may reach this oil break point in the next decade. If the United States can't break its dependence on imported oil, America will enter the uncharted waters of a new era of uncertainty and volatility.[34]

Iran, the world's fourth-leading exporter of oil, is becoming more and more belligerent toward the United States. Iranian president Mahmoud Ahmadinejad recently said, "Today, the time for the fall of the satanic power of the United States has come and the countdown to annihilation of the emperor of power and wealth has started. Iran…should get ready for a world minus the U.S."[35] America may have to take military action to stop Iran's nuclear program. Iran has promised the United States "harm and pain" if it takes any serious action against Iran's nuclear ambitions. Part of this harm and pain might come in the form of reduced oil exports. Though America does not import any oil from Iran, any substantial reduction in supply anywhere in the world will cause prices to escalate dramatically on world markets. Iran could also try to blockade the narrow Strait of Hormuz. Up to 40 percent of the world's oil flows out of the Persian Gulf through the strait every day. Any action against Iran by the United States or European nations or Israel could spark an interruption in the oil supply and a spike in prices unlike anything we can imagine.

As I mentioned before in *Armageddon, Oil and Terror,* if the oil break point is reached without adequate groundwork and readiness, U.S. national security will be compromised. The U.S. military machine runs on oil—lots of oil. Oil runs our jets, tanks, and troop transports. Without it, we are defenseless in conventional warfare. Without it, America cannot exert its military might on the world stage. In this scenario, all available fuel would have to be diverted to protect our nation. Strategic energy reserves would quickly be used up if the oil supply from the Middle East were disrupted. Even though we only get about 15 percent of our oil from the Middle East, if this pipeline were cut off abruptly, other nations would scramble to compete with the United States for alternate sources to offset their loss of Middle East oil. Drastic reductions in worldwide supply would affect everyone. Trucks that transport food, medicines, and other necessities would vie for the leftover and limited resources. Nonmilitary aircraft would immediately face severe fuel cutbacks. Normal commercial traffic would come to an abrupt halt. The U.S. economy would flatline.

The world is entering the long, dark tunnel of a new energy era. Only God knows what's at the end of the tunnel for our world and for America. Unquenchable thirst for oil may contribute to America's downfall.

ARE WE HEADED FOR AN ECONOMIC "PERFECT STORM"?

For years, Americans have reveled in profligate, load-up-the-back-of-the-SUV-at-Target excess, much of it paid for by credit cards, home equity or other loans. The binge has produced some supposedly healthy economic growth and provided everyone lots of nice stuff. But now debt collectors from around the world are knocking. That's why today's turmoil in U.S. financial markets will end in a massive transfer of wealth from America to the rest of the globe. The twenty-first century will overturn many of our basic assumptions about economic life. The twentieth century saw the end of European dominance of global politics and economics. The twenty-first century will see the end of American dominance too.

—*Time* Magazine

The headlines tell the story:

- "Nightmare on Main Street" (*Newsweek*, March 10, 2008)
- "The Great American Slowdown" (*Economist*, April 12, 2008)
- "Signs of a Growing Crisis: Relentless flow of bad economic news suggests there's no easy way out" (*USA Today*, July 16, 2008)

- "Seeing Shades of the 1930s" (*Newsweek,* July 28, 2008)
- "We Are All Socialists Now" (*Newsweek,* February 16, 2009)
- "Is the Almighty Dollar Doomed?" (*Time,* April 6, 2009)
- "G-20 Shapes New World Order with Lesser Role for U.S." (Bloomberg.com, April 3, 2009)

The long predicted meltdown finally hit in late 2008. It's been described as "Economic Armageddon." The aftershocks are reverberating through every area of the economy and America's debt now stands at an incomprehensible $14 trillion dollars. This indeed may be the beginning of the end and America could fall suddenly and sharply from its superpower status as a result.

It's the Economy, Stupid

In our world, money is god. In America, money is god. America's god has fallen on hard times. There's a Niagara of bad news. Rising oil prices. A war in Iraq that's cost at least $3 trillion with no end in sight. A subprime mortgage crisis and real estate implosion. Skyrocketing unemployment. Bank failures. The dollar under siege. Massive foreign investment in the United States.

Any way you slice it, America is in financial trouble. The world is enmeshed in a global economy, and bad news travels like toppling dominos, one problem quickly creating another. While economic fluctuations and trends are notoriously impossible to predict with any degree of accuracy, a consensus is growing that America's current woes aren't just part of the normal cycle of economic ups and downs.

America for Sale: Sovereign Wealth Funds

The economy and the burgeoning U.S. debt is dominating the headlines, but another aspect of America's financial woes is quietly moving front and center.

Sovereign wealth funds (SWFs) are front-page news. They are growing in both number and assets. The number of funds has doubled to forty just since 2000, and these funds are estimated to hold about $3 trillion in assets, which could shoot to $15 trillion by 2015. SWFs are "giant funds of money accumulated by the governments of wealthy countries in the Middle East and Asia, and used too late to bail out large U.S. banks."[1] They are "government-run investments financed by excess foreign reserves fueled by chronic trade surpluses."[2] They are owned mainly by major oil-exporting nations. Some maintain that SWFs could grow to $20 trillion in a relatively short time. The total debt and equity capital in the world is estimated at about $110 trillion. So, if SWFs do reach $20 trillion they "will be among the world's most important sources of investment capital."[3]

According to research conducted by the Peterson Institute for International Economics, the top four countries holding large sovereign wealth funds are the United Arab Emirates (worth a total of 500 billion USD), Norway (300 billion total), Kuwait (175 billion), and Russia (100 billion). To put this in perspective, the U.S. economy is estimated at around 13 trillion while the U.K. and China come in at just under 3 trillion. The relative size of SWFs gives the oil-rich nations that hold them a powerful influence over the world economy.

The concern is that these are nations that sell oil to America and then use some of that money to turn around and buy up American assets. Sovereign wealth funds invested an estimated $21.5 billion in U.S. companies in 2007. As the U.S. economy struggles, prices for foreign investors become cheaper and they can buy even larger chunks of America. There are indications that the shopping spree has already begun. Think about the list of investors who recapitalized Citigroup in recent months—SWFs from the Singapore, Kuwait, and Abu Dhabi governments. Incredibly, Asian investors bought a net $50 billion of U.S. stocks and bonds in January 2008 alone, up nearly 30 percent from the previous month. Charles Change, managing director of the boutique investment banking firm Accolade, in Seoul, notes, "The U.S. is getting pretty cheap."[4]

Michael Schuman, writing for *Time,* describes what's ahead as "America's coming garage sale."

> As the financial crisis in the U.S. persists, the combination of decreasing asset prices and a weakening dollar will make the U.S. cheaper and cheaper to foreign investors. Irresistibly cheap.... So all those dollars in banks around the world will flood back into the U.S. to buy stocks, bonds and property. Debt-burdened Americans, desperate for fresh cash, will be only too happy to sell—or be forced to sell. The U.S. will become one giant garage sale, where the buyers are Japanese banks, Chinese state-run investment funds and oil-rich Arab sheikdoms.[5]

While these funds do provide a beneficial source of capital for U.S. financial institutions, the growing fear is that the investment in and ownership of American companies by foreign nations will create a serious security threat— that they will get their hands on sensitive military information or even U.S. electric utilities, so they could simply turn off the power.

This concern first hit the headlines in 2006 with Dubai's proposed purchase of a British firm that serviced a number of key U.S. ports. The concern may have been overblown at the time, but it did highlight the growing danger on the horizon and spurred Congress to tighten the rules concerning foreign investment in the United States.

Chinese SWFs are of special concern to many in the United States. China wields its vast financial reserves as a political weapon. Whenever the United States raises concerns about China's currency manipulation or unfair trade practices, Chinese officials quickly resort to brass-knuckle tactics, threatening to dump their vast U.S. dollar reserves and stop purchasing U.S. bonds. This measure, often called a "financial nuclear strike," would lead to soaring interest and mortgage rates and would probably set off a U.S. recession.[6] Some have likened SWFs to a kind of Trojan horse strategy for taking over the United States. Others have a different take. They believe that allowing these nations to invest in America is actually giving the United States leverage over them because, no matter who might hold title to the assets, the assets physically rest on American soil and the United States could take them hostage by seizing them. One thing is for sure: America is being bought and sold—handed over to the highest bidder. And the buyer is more and more likely to come from one of the oil-producing nations.

Falling on Our Own Sword

When the first Arab oil embargo took place in 1973, the United States imported about 30 percent of its petroleum. As we saw in the last chapter, that number is now 70 percent and rising. America sends a staggering $600 billion a year overseas to buy oil from other countries, many of which don't like the United States. These nations have amassed staggering stashes of cash. This dynamic has reinvigorated Russia—whose economy was in shambles only ten years ago—and given them and many Islamic nations the stick with which they can turn around and threaten the United States.[7]

It's a dangerous game of numbers. Very…very large numbers. Economy-eclipsing numbers. Adam Davidson, an international and economics reporter for National Public Radio, provides some perspective:

> Earlier this week, the government of Abu Dhabi bought the single-largest ownership share of the massive U.S. bank Citigroup.… The government of Singapore has nearly half a trillion dollars that it is ready to spend on investments. Abu Dhabi has possibly more than $800 billion.[8]

How big are these numbers? Brad W. Setser of the Council on Foreign Relations says, "Half a trillion dollars is the amount of money that the U.S.

has to spend to import all the oil that it needs during an entire year, with oil at $100 [per barrel]."[9]

When asked if somebody with a trillion dollars could put the United States into a recession, Setser said, "Yes." And that's the mounting fear. These governments could use their huge investments to wreak havoc on the U.S. economy, or even on the world economy. Setser says it wouldn't be terribly difficult to pull off. They could slowly buy up a lot of U.S. dollars or U.S. treasury bills and then sell them all in one day.[10]

The United States is hemorrhaging economically and transfusing power and wealth to oil-producing nations like Russia, Saudi Arabia, and even Venezuela. Citgo is now owned by Venezuela and its incendiary, anti-American president, Hugo Chavez, who's been cavorting around with Iranian president Mahmoud Ahmadinejad. These nations know that oil is a finite resource and that the wealth won't last forever. So, by means of these sovereign wealth funds, they are buying the crown jewels of America at fire-sale prices. America needs the money, so it's auctioning off its own strength to those who will ultimately be aligned against it.

Tim LaHaye notes the prophetic significance of America's sell-off to SWFs and foreign investors:

> Right now China holds enough of our money that were they to
> exchange it for the Euro or some other monetary system, it would
> bankrupt our nation.... We read that some of our largest banks are
> going the way of the gas companies, which are by far the most prof-
> itable industries in America, showing over $30 billion profit in one
> quarter, and gasoline at the pump is continually going up. Shell is
> owned by Queen Juliana of Holland, one of the richest people in the
> world; BP is really British Petroleum; Citgo is owned by Hugo Chavez
> of Venezuela; Valero is owned by Mexico; Exxon and Standard are
> owned by that enthusiastic internationalist David Rockefeller (who

also owns the two largest banks in America plus media organizations). And one wonders who really owns America—foreigners or Americans?

This is not said to scare you, just to point out that the deck is already stacked in favor of a one-world economic system even before the Antichrist steps on the scene. Can you imagine how rapidly such a dictator could take over the reins of power after the rapture of the church?[11]

That's ultimately what's coming—a one-world economy led by the final world ruler. Events happening before our eyes are setting the stage for its appearance. But America's economic woes aren't all from the outside. We also have deep problems at home.

Life Takes Visa

The first widely accepted plastic charge card was issued by American Express in 1958. The first credit card that allowed balances to be paid over time was BankAmericard in 1959. Its name was changed to Visa in 1977. From this simple beginning, the credit card industry has mushroomed. Americans in 2006 possessed 984 million bank-issued Visa and MasterCard credit and debit cards. America's credit card debt has climbed to new records. A time bomb ticks in America's wallets.

- In 2007, household debt (including mortgages) totaled $14.4 trillion, or 139 percent of personal disposable income. In 2000, those figures were $7.4 trillion, or 103 percent of income. In other words, household debt doubled in seven years.[12]
- The average number of credit cards per consumer is four.
- 10 percent of consumers have more than ten credit cards in their wallets.
- The subprime meltdown involved about $900 billion in now-suspect securitized debt.

- U.S. credit card debt stands at a record $915 billion.
- Savings as a percentage of disposable income has dropped precipitously from 12 percent in 1980 to 0.4 percent in 2007, according to the Bureau of Economic Analysis.

David Rosenberg, chief North American economist at Merrill Lynch, sees trouble ahead. "What we have witnessed in the past 20 to 30 years—and especially the parabolic credit growth of the last five years—is going to be bursting in the next decade." *Time* business and economics columnist Justin Fox summarizes, "Americans simply don't have enough money to pay back the mortgage and credit-card debt they've run up."[13] And this debt on the personal level is amplified exponentially at the government level. States are in desperate trouble, with some teetering on bankruptcy. California is already there. And the U.S. government has racked up a debt that poses a grave threat to security.

How Empires Die

Debt is not just an economic issue. It also threatens the security—even the continued existence of nations. For instance, the U.S. Air Force says it needs more money to maintain the U.S. dominance of the skies that it's enjoyed for decades. The American military machine is aging due to the wars in Iraq and Afghanistan, and new fighters and new technology carry a bigger and bigger price tag. If the U.S. economy hits hard enough times, money allocations will have to be prioritized, hard decisions made. More of the limited funds going to entitlements and other government programs will mean less to defense and could leave the United States more vulnerable than ever in modern times.[14] Past empires have fallen under the crushing weight of massive debt service and their resulting inability to fund their military. As Niall Ferguson points out (*Newsweek,* December 7, 2009), Hapsburg Spain, Prerevolutionary France, the Ottoman Empire and even the British in the build-up to World War II all suffered the same fate. Several others have pointed out as well that the danger here is very real.

Welcome to Squanderville

Back in 2003 in an article in *Fortune,* Warren Buffett, the "sage of Omaha," predicted what we see happening. Buffet told the story of two fictional islands, Thriftville and Squanderville. The Squanderville residents lived beyond their means by importing from Thriftville in return for IOUs. Eventually, Thriftville converted this debt into Squanderville assets until Thriftville owned all of Squanderville. Buffet concluded his fable by warning that America was facing the same fate. Buffet said, "Our trade deficit has greatly worsened, to the point that our country's 'net worth,' so to speak, is now being transferred abroad at an alarming rate."

American is looking more and more like Squanderville every day.[15]

Danger on the Horizon

Among all of America's other economic land mines are runaway entitlements. In 2008, 28 million Americans received food stamps, including one in eight people in Michigan. How long can a nation survive economically when 10 percent of its population needs assistance just to put food on the table?

When 78 million baby boomers (that includes me) reach retirement age, the costs of Social Security and Medicare will skyrocket. This will leave the United States with unfunded promises of more than $50 trillion in today's dollars—equal to about three times the entire domestic product. That's about $175,000 for every American—and rising. To pay this, income taxes would have to double.[16] Medicare, which provides health care for 44 million seniors and people with disabilities, is forecast to spend more for hospital care in 2008 than it raises in taxes. Social Security will start spending money it's not earning as early as 2017 and will go bust in 2041 if Congress doesn't act.[17] Other experts concur that the genesis of the problem is in the fact that most Americans aren't worried at all by government spending or budget deficits and instead are focused on their own financial concerns.

I hesitate to issue any more bad news…but I will anyway: to all of the above we can add the metastasizing health-care costs that are running far ahead of the cost of living.

The Buck Drops Here

Any discussion about a future economic tsunami must take into account the ever-present terror threat. While sovereign wealth funds, oil prices, and U.S. debt might do in the American economy over the longer haul, there's a short-cut that could cause the U.S. economy to disintegrate. It's our worst nightmare—the WMD.

America must never forget that one of al Qaeda's persistent promises is to destroy the U.S. economy. And what better way to accomplish this quite-doable feat than by setting off a weapon of mass destruction (WMD) in a major American city. George J. Tenet, former director of the CIA, views this as the primary threat to America's future. But to pull it off, he says, "they would need to develop a plan as intricate as the 9/11 plot, most likely planned over a long period of time by sleeper cells operating in the United States."[18] Are they already here? How soon could it happen?

The American apocalypse is becoming a horrifying probability. We'll talk more about this in the next chapter.

OUR WORST NIGHTMARE:
ISLAMIC TERROR
AND A NUCLEAR 9/11

*I do know one thing in my gut: al Qaeda is here and
waiting. They understand that bombings by cars,
trucks, trains and planes will get them some headlines,
to be sure. But if they manage to set off a mushroom cloud,
they will make history. My deepest fear is that
this is exactly what they intend.*

—George Tenet, former CIA director

*Terrorists pose the most dire threat to
American security today. The "gold standard in terror,"
according to expert Daniel Benjamin, remains
"mass casualty attacks against Americans."*

—Nina Hachigian and Mona Sutphen, *The Next American Century*

*Washington is laid to waste. The capital is a blackened,
smoking ruin. The White House has been razed. Countless
thousands are dead. This is the apocalyptic scene terrorists hope to
create if they ever get their hands on a nuclear bomb.*

—*UK Daily Mail*

A "doom boom" is thriving in America. Our pop culture has gone apocalyptic. Some have called it "apocalypse new" and wondered with amazement "why we can't wait for the end of the world."[1] Look around. All kinds of apocalyptic visions surround us. The cinema blockbuster *I Am Legend,* starring Will Smith, is set in New York City after a genetically modified virus kills most humans and alters others into wild, vampirelike monsters. Cormac McCarthy's bestseller *The Road* is a post-apocalyptic novel set in the ravaged landscape of postnuclear America. The hit television series *Jericho* chronicles the lives of the people of Jericho, Kansas, after a nuclear strike cripples the United States. Even the hard rock group Nine Inch Nails has caught apocalypse fever. Their concept album *Year Zero* is set in 2022—a time of nuclear winter and no freedom. And the prototype for all these recent versions of the world's end was the Mad Max trilogy, which pictures the dystopia that remains after a worldwide oil shortage has led to nuclear war.

We seem to be fascinated by some collective vision that the world, and especially America, is prime for a nuclear nightmare. With the meteoric rise of radical Islam, loose nukes, and a Middle Eastern menace like Iranian president Mahmoud Ahmadinejad, this doomsday scenario hardly seems far-fetched today. America, which once seemed immune from the wars that have ravaged Europe and other continents, is now in the cross hairs of radical Islamists. America's strategic geographic situation no longer provides the firewall against attack that it did in earlier times. Jules Jusserand, the French ambassador to the United States from 1902–25, once observed that America is "blessed among the nations. On the north, she has a weak neighbor; on the south, another weak neighbor; on the east, fish, and the west, fish."[2] This may continue for quite some time to insulate America from direct attack by other nations. No plausible scenario envisions the continental United States being conquered and controlled by another nation via direct military attack. The U.S. military and arsenal of weapons is simply too stout.

Iraq is a perfect example of the difficulty of subduing and managing a medium-size nation that is geographically distant.[3] According to the 2006 Quadrennial Defense Review, the only nation that has any real chance in the near future of competing militarily with the United States is China. The U.S. intelligence community acknowledged in 2006 that China's missiles give it second-strike capability in any nuclear exchange with the United States. China has about 110 nuclear-armed missiles, including about 20 ICBMs (intercontinental ballistic missiles) that can reach any target in the United States.[4] They also have nuclear-powered submarines that each carry 16 ballistic missiles with a range of eight thousand kilometers (one-fifth of the world's circumference). This upgraded capability now gives China the ability to hit large portions of the continental United States from areas as far away as the Chinese coast. China's nuclear arsenal is certainly holding the attention of American military leaders. As one bumper sticker poignantly reads, "Even one nuclear bomb can ruin your whole day."[5]

But many argue that China's military is no match for the U.S. military in a head-to-head confrontation. Nina Hachigian and Mona Sutphen give this glowing appraisal of U.S. military superiority:

> The final reason the U.S. is not vulnerable to a traditional invasion or large-scale attack is precisely its uniquely capable military, which can take the fight to its enemy, wherever it is. The U.S. armed forces are so mighty that they defy comparison and even description. Never before in modern history has a great power's military been so vastly superior to that of its contemporaries. The U.S. spends more on its military each year than the rest of the pivotal powers combined, and roughly half of what the entire world spends. Washington's nonwar military budget, around $500 billion, is twice the size of the Russian federal government's entire 2008 budget and roughly five times the size of China's 2007 defense budget. This gulf is mirrored in every consequential measurement of military power, be it R&D, hardware, training, logistics,

information warfare, sustaining troops in theater, or command and control capabilities.... A head-to-head comparison of China's military with that of the U.S. is like comparing a rusty old pickup to an eighteen-wheeler.[6]

While America seems reasonably safe from direct invasion and conquest, the vulnerability to terrorism has already been horrifyingly demonstrated. Small groups of terrorists, rather than big countries, are the greatest threat to America for the foreseeable future. And most of our leaders believe it's a matter of *when*, not *if*, the next terrorist attack will occur. And they believe it will involve weapons of mass destruction.

It's very possible that the total absence of any scriptural reference to America in the end times is evidence that the United States will have been crippled by a nuclear attack or some other form of WMD. In the post-9/11 world, the detonation of a dirty bomb, nuclear device, or biological weapon on U.S. soil is a dreaded, yet distinct, probability. When it happens—and it appears that it's only a matter of time—the United States could be eliminated as a major player in international affairs. Such an attack could kill millions of people, trash the economy, and reduce the United States to a second-rate power overnight. Hachigian and Sutphen, in their excellent book *The Next American Century*, say, "The most dire potential threats to American security are a large-scale terrorist incident with a weapon of mass destruction, particularly a nuclear weapon.... Each of these dire threats has the potential to cause disruptions so massive as to alter life in the United States as we know it."[7]

How Real Is the Threat?

In the hotly contested 2004 American presidential election, President George W. Bush and Senator John Kerry disagreed on just about everything, but they did agree on one fundamental point. In the first televised debate between the two candidates, they were asked, What was "the single most serious threat to the national security of the United States?" President Bush, answering second, said, "I agree with my opponent that the biggest threat facing this country is weapons of mass destruction in the hands of a terrorist network."

Since 9/11 this has been America's gravest fear. Yet many seem to still doubt that it's possible. People find it difficult to believe that America-haters hiding in caves could really get WMDs and pull off a nuclear attack on U.S. soil.[8] But those who have examined the terrorist-WMD connection don't entertain any doubt. George Tenet, the former director of the CIA, says that, in the post-9/11 interrogations, "what we found stunned us all. The threats were real. Our intelligence confirmed that the most senior leaders of al Qaeda are still singularly focused on acquiring WMD.... The assessment prior to 9/11 that terrorists were not working to develop strategic weapons of mass destruction was simply wrong. They were determined to have, and use, these weapons."[9]

Osama bin Laden believes that the Islamists' religious faith obligates them to acquire nuclear weapons. When asked if he had nuclear or chemical weapons, bin Laden was quoted in *Time* magazine (December 24, 1998) as saying, "Acquiring weapons for the defense of Muslims is a religious duty. If I have indeed acquired these weapons, then I thank God for enabling me to do so." Suleiman Abu Gheith is an Islamic cleric from Kuwait and an al Qaeda spokesman. He posted a stunning statement on the Internet in June 2002, saying that "al Qaeda has the right to kill four million Americans, including one million children, displace double that figure, and injure and cripple hundreds of thousands." He arrived at these numbers by some sort of evil extrapolation from his calculation of the number of Muslims killed and maimed by the United States.[10] A senior al Qaeda paramilitary trainer, Ibn al-Shaykh al-Libi, told some Egyptian interrogators (and then later recanted) that al Qaeda had "collaborated with Russian organized crime to import into New York 'canisters containing nuclear material.'"[11] Sultan Bashiruddin Mahmood was the former director for nuclear power at Pakistan's Atomic Energy Commission. Many of his former colleagues considered him to be a madman. It's believed that he met in August 2001, about a month before 9/11, with Osama bin Laden and Ayman al-Zawahiri (al Qaeda's number-two man) in Afghanistan. He claims that he provided bin Laden with a bomb design. According to Mahmood, when he told bin Laden that the most challenging part of the process was obtaining fissile material, bin Laden said, "What if we already have the material?" Mahmood didn't know if bin Laden was bluffing or not, but he said that bin Laden's comment surprised him.[12]

In light of the gravity and frequency of these kinds of statements, growing concern is justified in the United States, "and the intelligence community is 'extremely concerned' with accumulating evidence that terrorists intend to use WMDs in attacks against the United States."[13] As far back as 1993, bin Laden was trying to get his hands on uranium in Sudan and was willing to pay $1.5 million to acquire some.[14]

Make no mistake. The threat is real. And it's growing every day.

Senate Statistics

The Senate Foreign Relations Committee surveyed analysts around the world in late 2004 and early 2005 to ascertain what they believed was the potential threat posed by weapons of mass destruction. The study was commissioned by the committee chairman, Senator Richard Lugar, who released this statement: "The bottom line is this: For the foreseeable future, the United States and other nations will face an existential threat from the intersection of terrorism and weapons of mass destruction."[15]

Employing a poll of eighty-five nonproliferation and national security experts, the authors of this report estimated the risk of attack by WMDs was considered to be as high as 70 percent by the year 2015. Most of the experts surveyed believed one or two new countries would acquire nuclear weapons by 2010, with as many as five joining the nuclear club by 2015. In other words, the spread of nuclear weapons is a serious problem that will be difficult to contain.

The survey report also contained these findings:

- The most significant risk of a WMD attack is from a radiological weapon, the so-called dirty bomb, in which radioactive material is put into a conventional explosive device.
- The threat that a dirty bomb will be detonated somewhere in the world by 2015 was judged to be 40 percent.
- The next highest risk is an attack with a chemical or biological weapon.
- The risk of attack with conventional nuclear weapons was judged to be 16.4 percent by 2010 and 29.2 percent by 2015.[16]

The world is only in the first decade of the age of terror, and the unthinkable has already happened in the well-orchestrated September 11, 2001, attack on U.S. soil. Just imagine what could loom on the horizon. Terrorist cells are multiplying all over the world. A major terrorist attack could hit any day. And the consequences are staggering.

The Failure of Imagination

In the aftermath of the 9/11 attack, a bipartisan 9/11 Commission was established to examine various aspects of the attack. Among its many findings, its major conclusion was that "failure of imagination" was primarily to blame for failure to prevent the September 11 attack. A similar failure of imagination leads many today to discount the risk of a nuclear 9/11.[17] But when Khalid Sheikh Mohammed, the chief planner of 9/11, first proposed an easier plan to charter a small plane, fill it with explosives, and crash it into CIA headquarters in Langley, Virginia, Osama bin Laden replied, "Why do you use an axe when you can use a bulldozer?"[18]

George J. Tenet served as director of the CIA for more than seven years (December 1996–June 2004). In 2007 he authored a 550-page book titled

At the Center of the Storm. Tenet believes that al Qaeda has begun recruiting non-Arab jihadists as a result of the United States' focus on Arab young men: "I am convinced the next major attack against the United States may well be conducted by people with Asian or African faces, not the ones that many Americans are alert to." Tenet says his deepest fear is "the nuclear one" and that Osama bin Laden and his operatives desperately want nuclear capability.[19]

Another frightening fact that is often overlooked in the nuclear discussion is that, according to a report from the National Defense University, about two-thirds of Russia's six hundred metric tons of bomb-ready nuclear material remains unsecured. That's enough for "tens of thousands of nuclear weapons."[20] For the right price, could jihadists get their hands on this material? Pakistan is also a growing problem. A. Q. Khan, the founding father of Pakistan's nuclear technology, was responsible for selling valuable nuclear technology to Iran, Iraq, North Korea, and Libya. The design for Iran's more advanced P-2 centrifuges ("P" is for Pakistan) came from Khan. Pakistan, an Islamic nation, is politically unstable yet has a nuclear arsenal of about fifty weapons. If Pakistan's nuclear capabilities were to fall into the wrong hands, "failure of imagination" could be an understatement.

Graham Allison, director of Harvard University's Belfer Center for Science and International Affairs, paints this sobering portrait of a nuclear attack on U.S. soil:

> On a normal workday, half a million people crowd the area within a half-mile radius of New York City's Times Square. If, in the heart of midtown Manhattan, terrorists detonated a ten-kiloton nuclear bomb (the yield of the bomb an intelligence source codenamed "Dragonfire" claimed was in New York one month after 9/11), the blast would kill them all instantly. Hundreds of thousands of others would die from collapsing buildings, fire, and fallout in the hours and days there-

after.... Furthermore, the effect of a nuclear terrorist attack would reverberate beyond U.S. shores. After a nuclear detonation, the immediate reaction would be to block all entry points to prevent another bomb from reaching its target. Vital markets for international products would disappear, and closely linked financial markets would crash. Researchers at RAND, a U.S. government-funded think tank, estimated that a nuclear explosion at the Port of Los Angeles would cause immediate costs worldwide of more than $1 trillion and that shutting down U.S. ports would cut world trade by 7.5 percent.[21]

Allison notes that "in the judgment of former U.S. Senator Sam Nunn, the likelihood of a single nuclear bomb exploding in a single city is greater today than at the height of the Cold War." In Allison's judgment, on the current trend line, the chances of a nuclear terrorist attack in the next decade are greater than 50 percent. He states that former Secretary of Defense William Perry believes Allison underestimates the risk.[22]

Graham Allison also comments on the grave risk America faces:

From the technical side, Richard Garwin, a designer of the hydrogen bomb, whom Enrico Fermi once called "the only true genius I had ever met," told Congress in March that he estimated a "20 percent per year probability with American cities and European cities included" of "a nuclear explosion—not just a contamination, dirty bomb— a nuclear explosion." My Harvard colleague Matthew Bunn has created a probability model in the Annals of the American Academy of Political and Social Science that estimates the probability of a nuclear terrorist attack over a ten-year period to be 29 percent— identical to the average estimate from a poll of security experts commissioned by Senator Richard Lugar in 2005.[23]

Allison concludes with this sobering equation: "Rather than quibble over percentage points, the bottom line is recognition that risk equals probability times consequences."[24]

Preparing for the Worst

A new study by researchers at the Center for Mass Destruction Defense (CMADD) at the University of Georgia details the catastrophic impact a nuclear attack would have on American cities.

> "The likelihood of a nuclear weapon attack in an American city is steadily increasing, and the consequences will be overwhelming," said Cham Dallas, CMADD director and professor in the UGA College of Pharmacy. "So we need to substantially increase our preparation."
>
> Dallas and co-author William Bell, CMADD senior research scientist and faculty member of the UGA College of Public Health, examined four high-profile American cities—New York, Chicago, Washington, D.C., and Atlanta—and modeled the effects of a 20-kiloton nuclear detonation and a 550-kiloton detonation. (For comparison, the nuclear bombs dropped on Hiroshima and Nagasaki were in the 12- to 20-kiloton range). Bell explained that a 20-kiloton weapon could be manufactured by terrorists and fledgling nuclear countries such as North Korea and Iran, while a 550-kiloton device is commonly found in the arsenal of the former Soviet Union and therefore is the most likely to be stolen by terrorists.

The study, which took three years to complete and appears in the current issue of the *International Journal of Health Geographics,* combines data on the impact of the devices, prevailing weather patterns, and block-level population

data from the U.S. Census Bureau to provide a level of detail previously unavailable.[25]

Here's just some of what they found:

> While the main effects from a 20-kiloton explosion would be from the blast and the radiation it releases, a 550-kiloton explosion would create additional and substantial casualties from burns. Such an explosion would superheat the blast zone, causing buildings to spontaneously combust. Mass fires would consume cities, reaching out nearly four miles (6.3 km) in all directions from the detonation site.[26]

As horrific as the physical consequences would be from any nuclear detonation on American soil, the psychological shockwaves would be equally ravaging. One wonders if the American psyche (or the psyche of any nation) could ever recover from the shock, devastation, and sense of helpless vulnerability that would result from such an action.

Calculating the Odds

Some maintain that any attempt at a nuclear 9/11 would have about a 90-percent chance of failing or fizzling. While that may sound like good news, it means that there's a 10-percent chance it would work. And the devastation would be beyond belief. But even in the case of a misfire, the havoc would be substantial. Graham Allison notes, "If a terrorist's ten-kiloton nuclear warhead were to misfire (known to nuclear scientists as a 'fizzle') and produce a one-kiloton blast, bystanders near ground zero would not know the difference. Such an explosion would torch anyone within one-tenth of a mile from the epicenter, and topple buildings up to one-third of a mile out."[27] No nuclear scenario on U.S. soil is positive.

Why Do They Hate America?

In the days following September 11, one question came up over and over. Many continue to ask it today: Why? (Tragedies always raise this question.) Why would someone do something like this? What could possibly inspire such evil?

Many answers were given. U.S. foreign policy "meddling" in the Middle East. Muslim bitterness over the presence of seven thousand U.S. troops ("infidels") on Muslim soil in Saudi Arabia. Cultural differences between America and Muslim nations. American arrogance and prosperity. Islamic extremists who view America as the Great Satan or enemy of God.

While many of these factors no doubt contributed to the terrorist motivation, one reason eclipses all others:

Israel.

In a *Time* article titled "Roots of Rage," Lisa Beyer gets to the root of the hatred that many Arab and Islamic nations feel toward America:

> Certainly the greatest single source of Arab displeasure with the U.S. is its stalwart support of Israel: politically (notably at the U.N.), economically ($840 million in aid annually) and militarily ($3 billion more, plus access to advanced U.S. weapons). To a majority of Arabs, Israel, as a Jewish state, is an unwelcome, alien entity. Even to those who accept its existence, Israel is an oppressor of Arab rights; despite the Oslo peace process, it still occupies most of the Palestinian territories. Particularly egregious to Muslims is Israel's control over Islamic shrines in Jerusalem, the third most sacred city to Islam.... When it comes time to broker peace in the region, many Arabs are inflamed by the strong U.S. bias in negotiations. To Islamic fanatics, including bin Laden, the peace process is of course anathema; for them, Israel is a state to be destroyed, not to be bargained with. Bin Laden, a Saudi, speaks out frequently against Israel.[28]

Osama bin Laden, in his televised rantings, has made reference to the Zionist infidels and the Palestinian issue. Iranian president Mahmoud Ahmadinejad regularly spews out venomous hatred for Israel. Ironically, he denies the Jewish Holocaust but wants to repeat it.

This is truly amazing. It all comes back to Israel. Israel is the key. Israel today is the "Little Satan." Why is this so amazing? Because the Bible predicts that in the end times Israel will be regathered to its land and that it will be in the world spotlight.

What's the big deal about Israel? The modern nation didn't even exist until May 1948. The entire country is only about the size of New Jersey. The total population is only about 6.3 million, including just over 5 million Jews. It's not a great oil-producing nation, yet you can't read a newspaper, listen to the news, or read a news magazine without some reference to what's going on in the tiny piece of real estate. Why all the fuss over Israel?

The answer to this question is really quite simple: Israel is in the eye of the hurricane of great end-time events. It is at the heart of most of the biblical prophecies concerning the end times. It occupies center stage in God's drama of the ages. Israel is God's supersign of the end times.

Incredibly, one of the main prophecies concerning Israel in the last days is that Israel will be hated by the nations of the earth. This is what we see in today's headlines. The Bible presents the coming Tribulation period as a time of mounting opposition against Israel, climaxing in an attack by all the nations of the earth.

Zechariah 12:2–3 says, "Behold, I am going to make Jerusalem a cup that causes reeling to all the peoples around; and when the siege is against Jerusalem, it will also be against Judah. It will come about in that day that I will make Jerusalem a heavy stone for all the peoples; all who lift it will be severely injured. And all the nations of the earth will be gathered against it."

This is saying that the nations will be obsessed with possessing the city of Jerusalem but those who grasp for it will face disaster. Israel will be a heavy, jagged stone that will cut to pieces those who try to remove it from its place.

You can just see the frustration and hatred for Israel growing in our world today. America's ongoing support for Israel will continue to draw the anger of the jihadists. We will continue to be the Great Satan in their eyes. As the threats mount, the call for America to abandon Israel will grow louder, but we dare not remove our support. As we will see later, in chapter 10, America's faithful support for Israel has been one of the secrets to its national success and will be key to its future blessing as well.

Terror Inside the United States

On February 12, 2008, Imad Fayez Mugniyah, the longtime military commander of Hezbollah, was killed by a car bomb in Damascus, Syria. He was known within his circles as Big Brother or the Fox. While no one took responsibility for the assassination, it's widely believed that the Israeli Mossad was behind it. That both the United States and Israel were after him is well documented. Mugniyah topped the United States' and Israel's most-wanted lists for a quarter of a century. The United States had placed a $5 million bounty on his head.

After Mugniyah's assassination, Hezbollah leaders in Lebanon and Iran immediately leveled numerous threats against Israel, calling Israel, among other things, a "cancerous germ." But there were also veiled threats against the United States. It's widely believed that Hezbollah has several cells in the United States. After Mugniyah's assassination, Hezbollah leader Hassan Nasrallah videotaped a message that was broadcast on giant television screens to thousands gathered in the huge Martyrs' Mosque. Nasrallah called for renewed attacks *beyond* Lebanon and even beyond Israel. This has been interpreted by many as a reference to the United States. But the chilling part is that after his call, the crowd inside the mosque thundered with their response: "At your service."[29]

Hezbollah is the surrogate of Iran. With Iran's steady march toward the nuclear finish line, Hezbollah could be the intermediary that Iran uses to unleash a nuclear surprise attack against the United States and bring down the Great Satan.

Five Minutes to Midnight

In 1947, scientists created something called the Doomsday Clock to symbolize the countdown to nuclear holocaust. The Bulletin of the Atomic Scientists' Doomsday Clock predicts how close humanity is to the figurative midnight of destruction. The hands on this clock have been pushed back and forth eighteen times since 1947.

In 1953, amid times of great uncertainty and fear, the hands were set at 11:58 after the United States tested a hydrogen bomb.

On November 27, 1991, the cover of the *Bulletin of Atomic Scientists* showed the hands on the clock pushed back to 11:43, the farthest they'd been from "nuclear midnight" since 1947. The reason for this optimism was stated in an accompanying editorial: "The Cold War is over. The 40-year-long East-West nuclear arms race has ended."[30]

But in May 1999, after India and Pakistan set off nuclear blasts, the hands were advanced to 11:51—nine minutes before midnight. Since that time, the hands have moved closer and closer to doomsday. In 2002 the clock was set at seven minutes to midnight, and since 2007 has stood at five minutes to midnight. Much of the recent concern is focused on North Korea, and even more on Iran.

Yes, the human race has its clock signaling our progress toward the end of the world. But don't forget that God has a clock too, and no one except God knows how close the hands on His clock are to midnight. At times like these, it's wonderful to remember that God is in control. He really does have the whole world in His hands.

7

WHEN GOD ABANDONS A NATION

*Your Republic will be as fearfully plundered and
laid waste by barbarians in the twentieth century as the Roman
Empire was in the fifth century, with this difference—
the Huns and Vandals who ravaged the Roman Empire came
from without, and your Huns and Vandals will have
been engendered within your own country.*
—Thomas Macaulay, British Parliamentarian, 1857

*American culture is complex and resilient.
But it is also not to be denied that there are many aspects
of almost every branch of our culture that are worse
than ever before, and that the rot is spreading.*
—Robert Bork, *Slouching Towards Gomorrah*

God is love.

There's no more comforting, reassuring truth in the world than that.
The God of the Bible is a God of compassion, kindness, grace, and mercy.
More songs, hymns, and poems have been written about God's love perhaps
than any other topic. People everywhere enjoy talking about the God who
loves the world. And rightly so.

We don't, on the other hand, like to talk about His judgment. The notion of divine judgment has never been popular. How many best-selling books expound on the wrath of God? But the truth remains that the loving God of the Bible is also infinitely just and righteous and, therefore, must express His wrath against human sin. No one can read the Bible honestly and escape this fact.

One often-overlooked aspect of God's judgment is His dealing with nations. God has often judged entire nations in the past. Lengthy sections in the Old Testament are devoted to God's prophesied judgment against nations. God repeatedly pronounced judgment against Judah and Israel for their disobedience. The majority of the Old Testament prophets are devoted to this subject—Isaiah, Jeremiah, Hosea, Joel, Amos, Micah, Zephaniah, Habakkuk, Zechariah, Haggai, and Malachi. But Judah and Israel were not the sole recipients of God's just displeasure. God also announced judgment on Gentile nations for their sin. Long catalogs of condemnation are found in all the major Jewish prophets—Isaiah 13–23, Jeremiah 46–51, and Ezekiel 25–32—listing nation after nation that has found itself under the mighty hand of divine wrath.

But there's more. Genesis 19 records the destruction of Sodom and Gomorrah and the cities of the plain for their gross sin. Ezekiel 16:49–50 gives the full reason for this divine judgment: "Behold, this was the guilt of your sister Sodom: she and her daughters had arrogance, abundant food and careless ease, but she did not help the poor and needy. Thus they were haughty and committed abominations before Me. Therefore I removed them when I saw it." As you can see, homosexuality was not the only "abomination" for which God judged Sodom, but it was the final straw.

God also judged Egypt, by means of a series of horrible plagues, for its failure to heed His command to let His people go (Exodus 5–12). The book of Nahum records God's judgment of the ancient Assyrian empire and its capital city of Nineveh in 612 BC for its violence, idolatry, pride, and selfish materialism. The brief prophecy of Obadiah is God's prediction of coming judgment on the kingdom of Edom for its arrogant sin against the Jewish people. The prophet Daniel (chapter 5) records the sudden fall of the Babylonian empire to the Medo-Persians in 539 BC.

In light of the biblical record, we would be shortsighted to believe that God no longer judges nations for their sin. Which raises a very important and often-asked question: will God judge America for its sin?

America the Beautiful

The founding and development of the American republic is legendary. Any tour of America's great historical monuments or reading of the founding documents reveals a deep awareness of the power and providence of the Almighty. One simply cannot escape the deeply religious, and frequently Christian, underpinnings of the American republic.

But it seems that, by any measure, America has begun a startling slide into moral decay. Estimates as to when the moral decline began may vary, but all the leading cultural indicators drive one to the conclusion that America is rotting from within.

There's hardly a need to quote a long list of statistics. Almost everyone sees it. Moral corruption on television, in movies, and at the newsstand. The covers of most popular women's magazines today, like *Glamour* and *Cosmopolitan*, are more explicit than the *Playboy* covers of the late 1950s. We see all around us evidence of our culture's "downward lemming-like rush."[1] Here are a few signs of the moral malaise in America.

- *Widespread acceptance of homosexuality promoted by the gay lobby.*
- *Abortion and the barbaric practice of partial-birth abortion.* About 50 million unborn babies are known to have been killed in the United States since the enactment of *Roe v. Wade* in 1973. And the Centers for Disease Control and Prevention (CDC) estimates that about 12–20 percent of the abortions performed nationwide are not reflected in their annual figures.

- *Pervasive Pornography.* The Internet has exploded its availability. It's a $10–$12 billion-a-year industry in the United States. Porn has become the norm.
- *Epidemic drug use and alcoholism.*
- *Raging sexual immorality and sexually transmitted diseases.* Here's a staggering statistic from the CDC that blew me away: 26 percent of American girls between the ages of fourteen and nineteen have at least one sexually transmitted disease.[2]
- *Unraveling of the family.* The United States has the world's highest divorce rate—currently twice what it was in 1960. "The risk of a marriage ending in divorce in the United States is close to 50 percent." At the same time, marriage rates are falling while cohabitation is on the rise. "From 1970 to 2004 the annual number of marriages per 1,000 adult women in the United States plunged by nearly 50 percent.... The number of unmarried, cohabiting couples has increased dramatically over the past four decades, and the increase is continuing."[3] This trend is hardly surprising in light of Hollywood's consistent mockery of the traditional family.
- *The national catastrophe of out-of-wedlock birth.* In 1948, only 3.8 percent of all women in the United States weren't married when they gave birth. In 1960, the number rose slightly to 5 percent. The number today stands near 40 percent. By 2015, it's projected to be 50 percent. At that point illegitimacy will be a greater factor in fatherlessness than divorce. In eight of America's forty largest cities, unmarried women give birth to more than three out of every five children.[4] "Out-of-wedlock births used to be a source of shame" and carried a social stigma, but now they're greeted with little more than a shrug. Surprisingly, according to the CDC, "teenagers account for only 23 percent of current out-of-wedlock births.... The vast majority of unwed mothers are old enough to know what they're doing.... Unwed

births are surging among women ages 25 to 29."[5] Again, Hollywood is setting the standard as more and more unmarried female megastars bear children.

America is hemorrhaging from within. The Huns and Vandals of moral rot are upon us. Herman Hoyt, a well-known Bible teacher, asks this searching question: "Within recent years, conditions within the country and criticism from without have raised the serious question of the continued greatness of this nation. Can this nation long endure with crime, lawlessness, and anarchy threatening from within...? Is this nation approaching dangerously near the point that other great nations reached before they disintegrated and disappeared?"[6]

I recently heard a man comment that the only way to promote morality in America is to convince Americans that "fornication is fattening." I'm not even sure that would work! In light of the moral drift in America, it's fitting to ask, Will God judge America?

The sobering answer appears to be that He has already started. The slide into the abyss has begun.

History's Pattern and Romans 1

History is strewn with the wreckage of many great nations that have risen to unusual power and influence, only to decline and fall under their own weight because of internal corruption, compromise, and a collapse of political will. It may well be that the United States today is at the apex of its power, just as Babylon was in the sixth century BC, prior to its sudden downfall in one night at the hands of the Medes and the Persians (Daniel 5). Any reasonable appraisal of moral conditions in the world today would justify divine judgment on any nation, including that of the United States. God is long-suffering and has blessed America with extraordinary benefits, including political and religious freedom and economic blessing. But one could argue that

America has squandered its birthright and that judgment is long overdue. The question is no longer *if* America deserves judgment but rather why a wasteful nation that is so richly blessed has been spared from divine judgment for so long.[7]

Romans 1:18–25 sets forth the character and cause of God's judgment against a civilization. In short, these verses tell us that when people willfully reject God, He eventually reveals His wrath against them. People can't turn their backs on God with impunity. Notice the very first line says that the wrath of God "is revealed," present tense. It's being revealed right now.

> For the wrath of God is revealed from heaven against all ungodliness and unrighteousness of people who suppress the truth by their unrighteousness, because what can be known about God is plain to them, because God has made it plain to them. For since the creation of the world his invisible attributes—his eternal power and divine nature—have been clearly seen, because they are understood through what has been made. So people are without excuse. For although they knew God, they did not glorify him as God or give him thanks, but they became futile in their thoughts and their senseless hearts were darkened. Although they claimed to be wise, they became fools and exchanged the glory of the immortal God for an image resembling mortal human beings or birds or four-footed animals or reptiles.
>
> Therefore God gave them over in the desires of their hearts to impurity, to dishonor their bodies among themselves. They exchanged the truth of God for a lie and worshiped and served the creation rather than the Creator, who is blessed forever! Amen. (NET)

Next, notice in Romans 1:26–32 *how* the wrath of God is revealed—in giving people over to the ravaging consequences of their sin:

For this reason God gave them over to dishonorable passions. For their women exchanged the natural sexual relations for unnatural ones, and likewise the men also abandoned natural relations with women and were inflamed in their passions for one another. Men committed shameless acts with men and received in themselves the due penalty for their error.

And just as they did not see fit to acknowledge God, God gave them over to a depraved mind, to do what should not be done. They are filled with every kind of unrighteousness, wickedness, covetousness, malice. They are rife with envy, murder, strife, deceit, hostility. They are gossips, slanderers, haters of God, insolent, arrogant, boastful, con-trivers of all sorts of evil, disobedient to parents, senseless, covenant-breakers, heartless, ruthless. Although they fully know God's righteous decree that those who practice such things deserve to die, they not only do them but also approve of those who practice them. (NET)

As you read these verses, did you catch the threefold repetition of that phrase "God gave them over" (verses 24, 26, 28). The word for "give over" or "hand over" is an intense Greek word: *paradidomi*. It's used in the New Testament for giving one's body to be burned (1 Corinthians 13:3). Three times it's used concerning Christ giving Himself up to death. Elsewhere it's used of someone being handed over to prison or judgment and of rebellious angels being handed over to pits of darkness.

There are two main schools of thought regarding this idea of God hand-ing people over to sin in Romans 1. The first and most common interpreta-tion is that God simply permits them to have their own way and suffer the tragic consequences of their actions—the simple, passive withdrawal of divine influence. William Hendricksen adopts this view; in his translation of Romans 1, people are "allowed by God to be swept away by their own sins into the pit of their vile passions."[8] I like the poignant way Frédéric Godet put it: "[God] ceased to hold the boat as it was dragged by the current of the river."[9]

While that view is certainly possible, I hold a second position, which is similar to the first but goes a step further. It sees God as *actively* handing people over to their sin and its consequences. The term *hand over* is used in the Old Testament to show God handing Israel over to its enemies to be defeated in battle. New Testament scholar Douglass J. Moo says, "But the meaning of 'hand over' demands that we give God a more active role as the initiator of the process. God does not simply let the boat go—he gives it a push downstream. Like a judge who hands over a prisoner to the punishment his crime has earned, God hands over the sinner to the terrible cycle of ever-increasing sin."[10] This doesn't mean that God sends a man into this self-destructive feedback loop at the very first instance of rebellion. God is long-suffering, merciful, and patient. Rather, this passage is saying that at some point the rebellious heart crosses a line, bursting through the limits of God's patience. That's when God will push the person downstream to the consequences of his or her own choices. It's more than just the removal of God's hand; it's His active handing over to sinful choices.

This reminds me of my boyhood, when my dad would take my brother and sister and me to Will Rogers Park in Oklahoma City. My favorite attraction was the slide. It was old and a little rusty, so it didn't give a very fast ride. But my dad would bring along waxed paper for me to sit on and would use other waxed paper sheets to rub on the slide and "grease the skids." As he pushed me down the slide, he wasn't just turning me over to gravity and the natural consequences of my choice to go down the slide. He was giving gravity some help, actively handing me over to it and giving me a push along my chosen path down the slick surface.

According to Romans 1, that's what God eventually does with nations or societies as well as with individuals: He judges them by handing them over to their sin. He greases the skids and pushes them on their way down to the bottom.

As well-known theologian R. C. Sproul notes, "When men refuse to honour God, they begin to dishonour themselves. Wherever the glory of God is attacked, sooner or later the dignity of man suffers. Since man is created in the image of God, there is a very real sense in which as God goes, so goes man."[11] Someone once said, "Whenever men lose God, they lose themselves."

But where is the line of judgment, the point at which God turns a nation over to its sin? When does the moral drift become so bad that God discloses His wrath? What are the signs that this has happened in a nation? Does Romans 1 give us any clues as to how close our nation might be to the tipping point, if not already past? I believe it does.

The Downward Spiral

In the three repetitions of the phrase "God gave them over" in Romans 1:24, 26, and 28, many respected commentators see a downward progression[12]— a kind of three-step process that is evident when God hands a nation over to the consequences of its sin. Let's look at these three steps.

Step 1—Sexual Revolution

The first signpost that God has turned a nation over to its own sin is rampant sexual immorality, or what we might call a "sexual revolution." We see this in Romans 1:24: "Therefore God gave them over in the sinful desires of their hearts to sexual impurity for the degrading of their bodies with one another" (NIV).

In other words, God allows people to plunge into the full depths of their hedonism, attempting to satisfy their inner hungers and cravings apart from Him.[13] When men and women abandon God, He abandons them, and the first indication that this has happened is overt sexual impurity. Of course, every nation in human history has had sexually immoral citizens. But sexual revolution arrives when God completely turns people over to their lusts, removing the outward restraints and allowing them to rush wantonly downward. When the true God is dismissed and rejected, the mental and spiritual vacuum that remains is quickly filled with all kinds of sexual sin.

According to a recent article in *Newsweek,* "TV sex has become more frequent—and much more graphic—in the past year."[14] Here are just a few of the new shows: Showtime has a program titled *Californication.* There's a sexually explicit soap opera, *Tell Me You Love Me,* and there are movies glamorizing sexual liberation, like *Sex and the City.* CBS aired a pilot in June 2008 titled *Swingtown* (as in "swingers" or wife swapping) that is "a frank exploration of sexual…liberation of the 1970s."[15]

Step 2—Homosexual Revolution

The second mark of a society abandoned by God is found in Romans 1:26–27: "For this reason God gave them over to dishonorable passions. For their women exchanged the natural sexual relations for unnatural ones, and likewise the men also abandoned natural relations with women and were inflamed in their passions for one another. Men committed shameless acts with men and received in themselves the due penalty for their error" (NET).

Unbridled practice of homosexuality and lesbianism, or what we might call a homosexual revolution, is the second sign that God has abandoned a nation.[16] Ray Stedman says, "Homosexuality is the second sign of a godless and wicked society. Paul says shameful lusts arise from inside, desires that are part of the soul of man. The apostle describes the rise of widespread psychological confusion.… When restraints are removed, homosexuality becomes widely accepted."[17] I agree with Stedman's description of the "psychological confusion" that we are witnessing firsthand. One hardly need say more. This is the USA today.

Respected Princeton theologian Charles Hodge writes, in reference to

Romans 1: "Paul first refers to the degradation of females among the heathen, because they are always the last to be affected in the decay of morals, and their corruption is therefore proof that all virtue is lost."[18] The explosion of lesbianism in America today is sad testimony to this fact. MTV features a bisexual reality romance show called *A Shot at Love 2 with Tila Tequila.* The CDC found that 11 percent of women ages fifteen to forty have had a same-sex sexual experience in their lifetime. Researchers said this was much higher than they expected.

Here are the results from a CDC survey that asked women, "Do you think of yourself as heterosexual, homosexual, bisexual, or something else?"

- 90 percent of women said they think of themselves as heterosexual.
- 1.3 percent think of themselves as homosexual.
- 2.8 percent think of themselves as bisexual.
- 3.8 percent think of themselves as "something else."
- Among women who have had sexual relations with another woman, nearly two-thirds (65 percent) consider themselves heterosexual.[19]

Apparently, more and more women who consider themselves heterosexual are experimenting with lesbianism as the walls of morality are being torn down. The number one song in America in July 2008 was "I Kissed a Girl" by Katy Perry. The song, which repeats the words, "I kissed a girl and I liked it," along with some other sad, confused lyrics, is about a heterosexual girl kissing another girl as an impulsive experiment. She hopes her boyfriend won't mind.

The homosexual lobby is working feverishly to gain acceptance for the homosexual lifestyle on par with acceptance of heterosexual intimacy. It's explicitly discussed on television, part of almost every sitcom. Even grade school children are forced to learn about it and discuss it. And not only have we lost our ability to be shocked, most people have become complacent, as if this were natural. In May 2008 the California Supreme Court struck down a law forbidding homosexual marriage. Same-sex marriage appears to be the wave of the future.

In the wake of the California Supreme Court decision to sanction gay marriage, Anna Quindlen said this in *Newsweek:* "Scream, shout, jump up and down. No matter. The gay-marriage issue is over and done with. The upshot: love won." She then added:

> If two women in white want to join hands in front of their families and friends and vow to love and honor one another until they die, the only reasonable response to that is happy tears, awed admiration and societal approval....
>
> Someday soon the fracas surrounding all this will seem like a historical artifact, like the notion that women were once prohibited from voting and a black individual from marrying a white one. Our children will attend the marriages of their friends.... The California Supreme Court called gay marriage a "basic civil right." In hindsight, it will merely be called ordinary life.[20]

Commenting on Romans 1, R. C. Sproul is crystal clear when he says that God "isolates homosexual behavior as the supreme loss of human dignity...the nadir of human corruption and dishonour."[21] He adds, "So one could say that the expansion, proliferation and explosion of homosexuality in a culture is in a certain sense a reflection of a demeaning view of man in general and an expression of the wrath of God upon that society."[22] With deep sadness, I agree. This is what's happening in America all around us. And the downward slide appears to be accelerating. In 1952, in what now appears an almost prophetic statement, well-known pastor Donald Grey Barnhouse said this concerning homosexuality in America: "There will be further efforts to bring our nation to a tolerant attitude toward this rebellion of sin.... Are men ignorant of the fate of

Sodom and Gomorrah?... Yet our civilization is on the same road. The evidences of this are overwhelming."[23]

One crucial point to understand in this discussion, which many Christians often overlook, is the key distinction between homosexual orientation and homosexual practice. If a person has an orientation toward those of the same sex, that's temptation. But if that person acts on his or her orientation by engaging sexually with a person of the same sex, that's sin.[24] As William Hendriksen says, "A person's sexual orientation, whether heterosexual or homosexual, is *not* the point at issue. What matters is what a person does with his sexuality!"[25] By missing this key distinction, many evangelicals diminish our credibility on this increasingly polarizing issue.

Also, we must never forget that God loves homosexuals. He loves all sinners and desires for them to turn from their rebellion and accept the forgiveness and transformation He offers through Jesus Christ (1 Corinthians 6:9–11). Christians should love homosexuals too. This has often not been the case and has hurt the cause of Christ. Admittedly, this is a fine line to walk for Christians, including me. It's very difficult to love people and yet strongly disapprove of their lifestyle, especially when we see the serious consequences for our nation. Yet, as homosexuality becomes more and more embraced, legalized, and sometimes even militantly protected, true believers in Jesus Christ must depend on the Holy Spirit for power and grace to be salt and light in our culture as we deal with this and other volatile issues.

Step 3—Openly Encouraging Evil

The third stage of the downward plunge for a nation is found in Romans 1:28–32:

> And just as they did not see fit to acknowledge God, God gave them over to a depraved mind, to do what should not be done. They are

filled with every kind of unrighteousness, wickedness, covetousness, malice. They are rife with envy, murder, strife, deceit, hostility. They are gossips, slanderers, haters of God, insolent, arrogant, boastful, contrivers of all sorts of evil, disobedient to parents, senseless, covenant-breakers, heartless, ruthless. Although they fully know God's righteous decree that those who practice such things deserve to die, they not only do them but also approve of those who practice them. (NET)

For our purposes, notice two key details in these verses. First, to be fair, one must note that the passage lists many sins besides sexual sins. We often focus only on sexual immorality and homosexuality in Romans 1:24–32 and overlook the catalog of other sins that serve as signs that God has abandoned a nation. It's true and significant that the first two signs of God's wrath against a nation involve sexual sin; they are clearly highlighted by God. But many other sins play a part in the unraveling of a civilization, as detailed in Romans 1:28–32. Sadly, all of these other sins are on open display in our culture as well.

Second, did you notice the final verse, the bottom rung of the ladder of abandonment? "They not only do them but also approve of those who practice them." The third step appears to be upon us, confirming God's desertion of the United States. Not only are we awash in moral filth, but we see overt, active encouragement of others to engage in the grossest forms of sin. Just watch any television talk show. Rarely is any perverse behavior criticized; often a call is issued to tolerate and accept it or even applaud it. For example, on April 3, 2008, Oprah Winfrey invited a pregnant transsexual on her program. Thomas Beatie had been transformed from female to male form but was now pregnant. A pregnant transsexual man. Celebrated on national television by Oprah. Wickedness has sunk to its lowest level when hearts are hardened to such an extent that they exploit and take delight in the sinfulness of others.

James Boice, the former pastor of the historic Tenth Presbyterian Church in Philadelphia, observes, "How do you appeal for good to a person who has become like that? Every argument you could possibly use would be reversed. The case is hopeless."[26] This is what we see more and more in public discourse in America. Any arguments against sin, especially sexual sin, are turned on their head, and the one who speaks out is made to appear narrow, ignorant, intolerant, and unloving. Evil is approved and encouraged while truth is mockingly scorned.

Like Looking in a Mirror

So when people ask, "When will God judge America?" the answer may well be, "He already is." The downward slide presented in Romans 1 mirrors what I've seen in my lifetime. I was born in 1959, near the end of the baby boom. I realize that all of us have a limited historical perspective, due to the brevity of our lives, and tend to exaggerate the events of our own time. But even with this self-awareness, I believe that the moral downgrade and coarsening of our culture during my lifetime is unprecedented. As a society, we've slowly removed God from our conscience, so God has given America over to these sins. Think about it. In the 1960s, America experienced a sexual revolution in which many of the restraints handed down from former generations were thrown off as antiquated shackles. Cohabitation, pornography, and open presentations of explicit sexual material now proliferate. I feel like I've been subtly desensitized, so that I easily shrug off evils that should trigger shame. If I, a man committed to Jesus Christ and His eternal values, have been so influenced by my culture, it's no wonder our nation is facing God's anger.

The sexual revolution of the 1960s was just the beginning—the first step, just as Romans 1 says. Not long after, America experienced a homosexual revolution as the homosexual movement began to spread into the mainstream as a viable alternate lifestyle. Television programs extolling the acceptability of active homosexuality and even homosexual marriage are now common. When I was growing up in the 1960s and '70s, homosexuality was considered wrong. Even non-Christians I knew believed it was wrong. But sometime in the 1980s a line was crossed. Homosexuality graduated from objectionable to ordinary. The second step of Romans 1 is being fulfilled before our eyes.

What's Ahead?

Well-known pastor and Bible teacher John MacArthur Jr., of Grace Community Church in California, has developed the concept of the "wrath of abandonment" from Romans 1. MacArthur recorded a program that aired on *Focus on the Family* in 2007, in which he summarizes much of what we've said:

> I don't believe we're waiting for God's wrath in this society. We haven't had a massive calamity such as the destruction of an entire city. We certainly don't want that to happen—pray that does not happen— but it could happen. And God would be just in any calamity that he brought upon us. We have not entered into eschatological wrath; that comes in the end times. We are experiencing—all of us do—consequential wrath of sin. But this massive concept of the wrath of abandonment, I'm convinced, is now at work in our society. We like to talk about the fact that America was founded on Christian principles, God was at the center of it, and all of that—whatever it might have been in our founding, it's no longer the way it is.… The first thing that happens in a nation when it has been abandoned by God is a sexual revolution. Moral sexual perversion, pornographic desire describes the general character of the culture. You can't even count how many million pornographic websites there are. When a society is abandoned by God, it operates out of its own perverse sexual passion without restraint.

MacArthur concludes:

The second step in the progression, [Romans 1] verse 26: "God gave them over"—not just to passions that are explicable, because they're men and women, but to inexplicable—"degrading passions; for their women exchanged the natural function for that which is unnatural." You know a society has been abandoned by God when it celebrates lesbian sex. God has given them over—gross affections, unnatural, unthinkable. So you follow a sexual revolution with a homosexual revolution. And homosexuality becomes normalized.

MacArthur is not alone in this view. Dr. S. Lewis Johnson, former pastor of Believers Chapel in Dallas and professor of New Testament at Dallas Theological Seminary, says this about Romans 1 and its application to America today:

Today films, plays, clubs, now even churches and ministers apologize for, and even glorify, the unnatural practices that the Bible speaks about both here and elsewhere. I'd like for you to notice carefully what Paul is saying. He's not saying that we are in danger of judgment. That is not Paul's theory at all. He is saying that these things that we are talking about, the spread of immorality, the spread of sexual sin against God, the spread of violence, the spread of crime, ARE the judgment of God. It is not that we are in danger of judgment, it is that these things are the judgment of God.... So our civilization is not in danger of contracting a fatal disease. Our civilization has already contracted a malignant and fatal cancer through its unbelief in the message of God in Christ. And we are hurrying on to the climactic destruction that is to come.[27]

I believe God is already judging America for its sin. The signposts of Romans 1 are at work in American culture. We are already in the process of being abandoned to the consequences of our chosen rebellion against God. It's tragic to witness, isn't it? Could God choose to move from this indirect means of judgment to a more direct means at any time? Of course He could. *Will* God judge America by means of some open, catastrophic disaster? I can't answer that question, and neither can anyone else. No one on earth knows for sure. We do know that God is long-suffering and patient with individuals and nations.

Fortunately, His timetable is not ours (2 Peter 3:8). And who's to say that God in His grace and mercy couldn't reverse the onset of judgment in response to widespread repentance and some form of modern Great Awakening? I don't profess to know God's plans in this arena. But I do believe we can say, from the Bible, that the process of Romans 1 seems to be at work in America today, and the rebellion seems to be deepening and intensifying. If this continues unabated, then a more open manifestation of God's judgment will certainly follow at some point. God must be true to Himself and His Word. If calamity comes, it could be part of the explanation for America's absence from biblical prophecy.

One of my friends used to say, "The darker the outlook, the better the uplook." Let's turn now from the outlook to the uplook. It may be something you haven't thought about very much. In a strange twist, God's final act of judgment against America could be an event that's commonly known as the Rapture.

8

THE RAPTURE:
THE END OF AMERICA
AS WE KNOW IT

The Rapture: The moment, predicted in Thessalonians,
when Jesus suddenly removes the faithful from the earth....
fifty-five percent of Americans think that the faithful
will be taken up to heaven in the Rapture.

—Newsweek

Imagine today's world if the United States were suddenly, for all practical purposes, eliminated from the global picture. Collapsing markets. Communications chaos. Trade and supply mayhem. And a massive power vacuum that other nations will rush to fill in a matter of hours.

I believe that biblical prophecy makes this scenario a real possibility for our near future. And it all revolves around one event of future history, an incomparable promised blessing for those who believe in Jesus Christ and a devastating blow to the United States and the world. Bible scholars call it the Rapture.

It appears that in God's timetable, America remains a key player until the Rapture occurs. It's after the Rapture that the Group of Ten come on the scene in Europe, along with the Antichrist, and negotiate the peace treaty that temporarily suspends the Middle East crisis. Up until that point it seems that America will continue to be Israel's key ally and defender. If that's true— if America must remain strong up to the time of the Rapture but afterward be replaced by Europe as the center of power and peace negotiations—then what does this tell us?

I believe the Rapture will bring America to its knees. The Rapture will change everything.

But what is the Rapture? Why will it have such a dramatic effect on geopolitics?

The Rapture Revealed

Simply stated, the Rapture of the church is that future event when Jesus Christ will descend from heaven to resurrect the bodies of *departed* believers and catch up every *living* believer (body, soul, and spirit) immediately into His glorious presence in a moment of time. He will then escort them to heaven to live with Him forever. All will instantaneously receive new, incorruptible, imperishable, immortal bodies that are fit for existence in heaven (1 Corinthians 15:35–49).

That's the Rapture in a nutshell.

The term *Rapture* is taken from 1 Thessalonians 4:17: "Then we who are alive and remain will be *caught up* together with them in the clouds to meet the Lord in the air, and so we shall always be with the Lord." In this verse, the words *caught up* translate the Greek word *harpazo,* which means to snatch, to seize, or to take suddenly or vehemently.

The word *harpazo* appears thirteen times in the New Testament (Matthew 11:12; 13:19; John 6:15; 10:12, 28, 29; Acts 8:39; 23:10; 2 Corinthians 12:2, 4; 1 Thessalonians 4:17; Jude 23; Revelation 12:5). Take a moment to look up these verses and you will see that *harpazo* is variously translated as "take forcibly," "snatch," or "caught up."[1]

While the Rapture is referred to many times in the New Testament, three main passages describe the Rapture of the church. Carefully reading each of these passages will help you get a basic overview of the Rapture directly from Scripture.

Do not let your heart be troubled; believe in God, believe also in Me. In My Father's house are many dwelling places; if it were not so, I would have told you; for I go to prepare a place for you. If I go and prepare a place for you, I will come again and receive you to Myself, that where I am, there you may be also. (John 14:1–3)

Now I say this, brethren, that flesh and blood cannot inherit the kingdom of God; nor does the perishable inherit the imperishable. Behold, I tell you a mystery; we will not all sleep, but we will all be changed, in a moment, in the twinkling of an eye, at the last trumpet; for the trumpet will sound, and the dead will be raised imperishable, and we will be changed. For this perishable must put on the imperishable, and this mortal must put on immortality. But when this perishable will have put on the imperishable, and this mortal will have put on immortality, then will come about the saying that is written, "Death is swallowed up in victory. O death, where is your victory? O death, where is your sting?" The sting of death is sin, and the power of sin is the law; but thanks be to God, who gives us the victory through our Lord Jesus Christ. (1 Corinthians 15:50–57)

But we do not want you to be uninformed, brethren, about those who are asleep, so that you will not grieve as do the rest who have no hope. For if we believe that Jesus died and rose again, even so God will bring with Him those who have fallen asleep in Jesus. For this we say to you by the word of the Lord, that we who are alive and remain until the coming of the Lord, will not precede those who have fallen asleep. For the Lord Himself will descend from heaven with a shout, with the voice of the archangel and with the trumpet of God, and the dead in Christ will rise first. Then we who are alive and remain will be caught up together with them in the clouds to meet the Lord in the air, and so we shall always be with the Lord. Therefore comfort one another with these words. (1 Thessalonians 4:13–18)

When the Rapture occurs, every living believer in Jesus Christ will be snatched off planet earth and whisked away to heaven in the amount of time it takes to blink your eye. It will be the most world-changing event since the world's destruction by the flood in the days of Noah.

The Day After the Rapture

Think about it: if the Rapture were to happen today, if all the true believers in Jesus Christ were whisked away to heaven in a split second, the world, and especially America, would be devastated beyond comprehension.

Consider these most recent statistics from Barna Research Online. Eighty-five percent of Americans claim to be Christians. This group is often identified as "cultural Christians" and includes many who consider themselves Christians simply because they belong to a "Christian" family or a "Christian" nation, or they believe a God exists, or they attend church semiannually or even regularly. Out of this majority, a distinct subset is often designated "born-again Christians"—that is, those whose faith is more than a mere label, whose lives have been truly transformed by genuine faith in Jesus Christ. According to pollster George Barna, looking back nearly two decades we find the percentages of born-again Christians holding steady between 35 and 42 percent. Barna estimates that America's population includes one hundred million born-again Christians, which he defines as "people who said they have made a personal commitment to Jesus Christ that is still important in their life today and who also indicated they believe that when they die they will go to heaven because they had confessed their sins and had accepted Jesus Christ as their savior."[2]

Barna identifies "evangelicals" as a further subset of born-again Christians meeting seven other conditions:

Those include saying their faith is very important in their life today; believing they have a personal responsibility to share their religious beliefs about Christ with non-Christians; believing that Satan exists; believing that eternal salvation is possible only through grace, not works; believing that Jesus Christ lived a sinless life on earth; asserting that the Bible is accurate in all that it teaches; and describing God as the all-knowing, all-powerful, perfect deity who created the universe and still rules it today. Being classified as an evangelical is not dependent upon church attendance or the denominational affiliation of the church attended.[3]

In 2007, 42 percent of Americans claimed to be "born-again Christians," while 8 percent of American adults were identified as "evangelical Christians."[4] The most distinctive factor in this category is the fourth in Barna's list of seven conditions—a belief that salvation is by faith in Christ alone, without human works. According to Barna, this represents about fourteen to sixteen million American adults. Adding in children, the number could easily climb to twenty-five to thirty million.

The total U.S. population, according to the 2000 census, was 281,421,906. In October 2006 it was announced that the United States passed the three-hundred-million mark. If Barna's 8–10 percent figure is close to reality, that means that, even by the most conservative criteria, at least 25 million Americans are believers in Christ or are small children of believers. Less restrictive estimates put the number as high as 65 million.

That's how many Americans will disappear, all at once, when the Rapture occurs.[5] The impact will be nothing short of cataclysmic. Not only will our country lose at least 10 percent of its population, but it'll lose the "salt and light" of this great land (Matthew 5:13–14).

No doubt, all kinds of wild explanations will arise for the phenomenon—alien abductions, some kind of polar shift, or new laser weaponry that zaps people out of existence. No matter how people try to explain it, one thing is for sure: the United States, with its substantial Christian citizenship, will be crippled.

The same cannot legitimately be said of any other nation in the world. Patrick Johnstone, in his book *Operation World,* gives the following statistics for the number of believers in various regions of the world.[6]

United States	32.5 percent
Asia	3.6 percent
Africa	14.8 percent
Middle East	less than 1 percent in most countries
Latin America/Caribbean	10.5 percent

The numbers for Europe are staggering. Johnstone and Mandryk note that for Europe the number is 2.4 percent. And this is the continent that produced the Protestant Reformation less than five hundred years ago!

The sparseness of believers in some parts of the world really hit home with me back in 1998 when I was traveling for study in Turkey. One night on a bus nearing Izmir, a city with a population of about three million, we topped a rise from which I caught a glimpse of the city shimmering in the night. As I looked around on the bus and surveyed the massive city, I thought to myself, *If the Rapture were to occur right now, these poor people would never know the difference.* You see, according to a Turkish pastor in Izmir who is a close friend, the entire city is home to only a few hundred true believers in Christ. A few hundred people out of three million. They would hardly be missed. The Rapture will be a blip on the radar screen for many nations and entire regions of the world.

But not so in America. The immediate ripple effect (or should I say "tidal wave effect"? There'll be no "rippling" involved!) will impact every area of our society. Think about what will happen to the Dow Jones the next morning.

The stock market will free fall. The NASDAQ will plummet. And talk about a mortgage meltdown. Millions of mortgages will plunge into irrecoverable default. America will be left reeling. And think about the other consequences. Military personnel by the thousands…permanently AWOL. Factory workers will never show up for work again. College tuitions will go unpaid. Businesses will be left without workers and leaders. The entire economy will be thrown into chaos.

Tim LaHaye and Ed Hindson address the unimaginable impact of the Rapture: "America in particular would suffer great loss because of the high percentage of Christians who live in the United States. Consider what happened to the city of New Orleans after Hurricane Katrina. The entire city was emptied within a few days, and much of it has yet to recover. Imagine such an impact on every major city in America."[7]

Charles H. Dyer, a well-known Bible teacher, wrote in 1991 (referring to that time's lower census figures):

> Today as many as half of all Americans claim to be "born again," or believers in Jesus Christ. If only one-fourth of that number have genuinely made a personal commitment to Christ, then over 28 million Americans will suddenly "disappear" when God removes his church from the earth.
>
> Can you imagine the effects on our country if over 28 million people—people in industry, government, the military, business, agriculture, education, medicine and communications—disappear? That is approximately double the entire population of New York City, Los Angeles, Chicago, and Houston all rolled together!
>
> The economic fluctuations of the eighties and even the Great Depression will pale in comparison to the political and economic collapse that will occur when our society suddenly loses individuals who were its "salt and light." America could not support an army in

the Middle East because the military would be needed at home to control the chaos![8]

The Rapture may well be the end of America as we know it. Those who miss out on the Rapture in the United States will be left behind to pick up the pieces. America will no longer be the world's superpower. The mighty USA will move from being a leading nation to a following nation.

The Rapture Could Be the Final Blow

While the Rapture will devastate the American economy in unimaginable ways, it doesn't appear that the Rapture alone could make America a second-rate power. After all, even if the Rapture were to happen today, America would still retain all its military muscle. The United States would lose thousands of troops and commanders, but the formidable American nuclear arsenal would remain intact and could be unleashed with the push of a few buttons. So while the Rapture will change everything in America and throughout the world, in all probability the withdrawal of the United States from the role of superpower and world policeman will result from the impact of not one but several events. One or more of the scenarios described in the previous chapters—oil starvation, economic collapse, WMD attack, or some other convergence of events—could put the U.S. economy into full cardiac arrest, devastate our military machine, turn America's attention inward upon itself, and provoke a mood of isolationism from world affairs.

When the United States is forced to abandon its role as the most dominant power in the world, the balance of power will shift quickly to Europe and the Middle East, just as the Bible predicts. These parts of the world will not be affected nearly as dramatically by the Rapture. The minimal impact of the Rapture on Europe, where biblical faith has seriously eroded, will leave the

European Union poised to lead the Western world. Power will shift dramatically away from the United States.

Could America fall before the Rapture? No one on earth knows the final answer to this question. But it appears to me that America will remain a key player up until the Rapture. Why do I say that? Think about it. America is Israel's key ally. If it weren't for the strong support of the United States, Israel would have been wiped out decades ago. And we know from the Bible that Israel will be a viable nation when the Tribulation begins. Israel has a powerful, formidable military machine, but up against Russia and all the Arab nations, it wouldn't stand a chance. America has provided the strong deterrent against any all-out onslaught against Israel.

But the Rapture could happen at any time, and after that, all bets are off. America's tragic fall could be coming soon.

AMERICA:
FROM SUPERHERO
TO SIDEKICK

*"America is not mentioned anywhere in the Bible, implying that
it would be crippled or taken out of the picture in some way."*
—Glenn Beck (April 2009)

Yes, it's sad to imagine the once-majestic, God-blessed, idealistic United States relegated to the convalescent home for has-been nations. Historians and loyalists during the demise of every great world power must have felt the same way. But is this picture a certainty? No. Just because America is not mentioned or referred to specifically anywhere in Scripture, one must be careful in drawing any hard and fast conclusions about the nation's future. Nothing on this subject can be stated with certainty.

However, in my study I have discovered a fairly broad consensus among prophecy scholars concerning the destiny of the U. S. The predominant view is that in the end times America will be absorbed into the Antichrist's reunited Roman Empire, becoming a part of the end-time Western confederacy of nations.

Charting America's Future

During the coming seven-year Tribulation, Scripture presents the world as divided into four main power blocs. These alignments of nations will rise and fall at different times, and for the last half of the Tribulation, the Antichrist will rule the world. Here are the four great last-days blocs of nations that are mentioned in Scripture:

1. The King of the North (Daniel 11:40)

   I believe this is a northern coalition of nations led by Russia. In Daniel 11:5–35 the historical king of the north was the leader of the Seleucid Empire centered in Syria but including a vast territory north and east of Israel. The prophetic counterpart to the Seleucid, or prophetic "king of the North" in Daniel 11:40, seems to be a great northern confederacy headed by Russia but including Iran and the nations of central Asia (see Ezekiel 38–39).

2. The King of the South (Daniel 11:40)

   This appears to be the leader of Egypt, who directs an Islamic league of nations centered in North Africa and the Middle East.

3. The Kings of the East (Daniel 11:44; Revelation 16:12)

   All that we know about these nations is that they come from east of the Euphrates River to gather at Armageddon for the final great conflict of this age. The kings of the East could include modern Afghanistan, India, Pakistan, China, Japan, or Korea.

4. The King of the West (Daniel 2:40–43)

   While the Antichrist is never actually called the "king of the West," as the leader of the reunited Roman Empire centered in Europe, this is an apt title for him. This king will lead the confederation of Western nations in the end times and will ultimately expand his empire to include the entire world during the final three and a half years of the Tribulation (Revelation 13:4–8).

While not every specific nation is mentioned in end-time prophecy, these are the four great future confederations of nations presented in Scripture. It appears that most of the nations of the world will be joined to one of these power blocs at one time or another.

Now, let me ask you a question: Which of these power blocs would the United States probably join when the nations of the earth shift and scramble for position after the Rapture, as new alliances form, as emerging leadership is called upon to quell the chaos? Where would we naturally gravitate? The Western alliance, right? Why? Because that's who we are strongly tied to today. Through its past roots and modern alliances, such as NATO, the United States is bound to the nations of Western Europe.

Now I want to let you hear from several well-known theologians and prophecy teachers who espouse this theory. I understand that their agreement doesn't prove the truth of what they say, but it does lend strong credence to the view that after the Rapture, America will end up in league with the Western confederacy under the Antichrist. Here's a small sample of those who represent this view.

Tim LaHaye and Ed Hindson write:

> The rapture will result in global political, social, and economic chaos. New alliances, political power shifts, and emerging leadership will have to attempt to restore law and order to the planet. This will pave the way for the Antichrist to rise to power, probably in Europe. The rapture would leave America as a second- or even third-rate power in the Western world, making it likely America could turn to Europe for leadership and stability.[1]

John Walvoord, often referred to as the "dean of modern Bible prophecy," also sees the United States in league with Europe in the end times.

> Although the Scriptures do not give any clear word concerning the role of the United States in relationship to the revived Roman Empire and the later development of the world empire, it is probable that the United States will be in some form of alliance with the Roman ruler.

Most citizens of the United States of America have come from Europe and their sympathies would be more naturally with a European alliance than with Russia or countries in Eastern Asia. It may even be that the United States will provide large support for the Mediterranean confederacy as it seems to be in opposition to Russia, Eastern Asia, and Africa. Actually a balance of power in the world may exist at that time not too dissimilar to the present world situation, namely, that Europe and the Mediterranean area will be in alliance with America in opposition to Russia, Eastern Asia, and Africa. Based on geographic, religious and economic factors, such an alliance of powers seems a natural sequence of present situations in the world.

If the end-time events include a destruction of Russia and her allies prior to the final period of great tribulation, this may trigger an unbalance in the world situation that will permit the Roman ruler to become a world ruler. In this event, it should be clear that the United States will be in a subordinate role and no longer the great international power that it is today. [2]

Charles Ryrie, a popular theologian and editor of the well-known Ryrie Study Bible, looks to America's European roots and heritage as a key clue to its future in the end times.

It is not too farfetched to envision the United States someday aligned with the Western Confederation of Nations which will be formed by Antichrist. National origin could be the link, since many United States citizens originally came from the countries which will make up that Western alliance of nations.

The United States has received a larger number of immigrants than any other country in history. The thirteen original states were settled mostly by colonists from the British Isles. In 1780 more than three-fourths of the American population were descendants from English and Irish settlers. The rest came from Germany, the Netherlands, France, and Switzerland.

Between 1841 and 1860 over four million newcomers found homes in the United States. Almost all came from Ireland, Germany, Great Britain, and France. In 1882 three out of every four immigrants came from northern and western Europe. By 1896 more than half the immigrants originated from countries in southern and eastern Europe, such as Italy and Austria-Hungary.

Ryrie concludes:

So when the European Federation of Nations rises to power, the United States may find herself in a supportive role in favor of this powerful alliance and in opposition to the other power blocs in Russia, Africa, and the Far East. This would mean that the United States, haven of Christianity for two centuries, will find herself in league with Antichrist. None of these options—third-rate power, desolated wasteland, or backer of Antichrist—paints a very bright future for the United States.[3]

Prophecy experts Thomas Ice and Timothy Demy come to the conclusion:

Thus, according to this way of thinking, the United States would be viewed as an appendage of the Revived Roman Empire. This would mean that the United States, with all its vast military and economic resources, would be aligned with the Revived Roman Empire and the Antichrist during the tribulation.... Such a scenario could be possible because this view would only require the United States to be an appendage of, but not one of, the ten nations in the Revived Roman

Empire. After all, every nation will have to be associated with one of the various entities outlined in the end-time prophetic plan.[4]

Ed Dobson, a well-known pastor and prophecy teacher, says, "But we know that when the Eastern coalition armies begin their invasion of Israel for the Battle of Armageddon, they will be opposed by the Antichrist and a coalition of Western nations (Revelation 16:12–14). The United States will most likely be part of that coalition because it is a Western superpower."[5]

I agree with this view. It makes the most sense from what I see in the Bible, from America's past, and from today's headlines.

The Slide from Sovereignty

The amalgamation of America into the Antichrist's European empire after the Rapture is not nearly as far-fetched as it used to be. In fact, it makes perfect sense in the current political climate. The United States is slowly, subtly, yet relentlessly being drawn away from national sovereignty into a globalist order. NATO, the UN, GATT, NAFTA, the WTO, and many other acronyms signal the startling trend away from U.S. sovereignty and toward our submission to multinational treaties, organizations, and courts of law.

Jerome Corsi, author of *The Late Great U.S.A.: The Coming Merger with Mexico and Canada,* maintains that the United States will be incrementally absorbed into a North American Union that will be fashioned after the model of the European Union. He cites evidence that a name has already been proposed for the new currency, called the "amero." This is certainly possible in the emerging new world order. Corsi presents a fairly convincing case. But none of us knows for sure. We may navigate many twists and turns before the dust finally settles. But in the end, the most logical final outcome for the United States, in light of the Bible and current events, is absorption into the Western coalition led by the future Antichrist.

Some Final Conclusions

The future of America that we can deduce from Scripture is exactly what we see beginning to materialize before our eyes in today's headlines. America is encountering serious problems at home and abroad. We're oppressed by a sense of some impending crisis.

When the trumpet sounds and all the believers in the United States vanish, America's final days will be like so many pages dangling from a December calendar. Like all the great powers before it, the United States will collapse under the weight of its own sin, self-indulgence, and excess.

In this light, here are the seven conclusions we have reached up to this point.

1. America is not mentioned in the Bible.
2. America is Israel's main defender.
3. It appears that America must remain strong until the end times to continue its defense of Israel as the Jewish state tries to stay afloat in a sea of enemies.
4. The scriptural silence concerning America in the end times (after the Rapture) indicates that America will fall from its position of world prominence.
5. World power in the end times is centered in the reunited Roman Empire (Europe).
6. European prominence can only be explained in light of U.S. decline.
7. The United States will suffer its decline and its fall at the Rapture of the church, probably in combination with a series of other harsh setbacks.

Where Do We Go From Here?

So, does this mean we should throw in the towel? Should we give up on America? God forbid! No one knows for sure what will happen to America or when it will happen. Therefore, we ought to do all we can to serve God's purposes as long as we can. As long as the Lord gives us breath, we should continue to do all we can for the spiritual well-being of our nation and the world. Even if the scenario we've developed is a true picture of our future, we don't know how long we have until the trumpet sounds and our opportunities to introduce people to Jesus Christ will end.

In the next chapter, let's consider a few specific ways we can secure the continued blessing of God upon our great nation as we await the Lord's coming.

OUR ROLE IN
GOD'S FOREIGN AND
DOMESTIC POLICIES

*What makes a nation great? Economic power?
Military might? The answer obviously depends on the standard
by which greatness is measured. If God delights in goodness,
generosity, and justice, then the nation that practices these
will be great in God's estimation. But there's more to greatness
than these things. God has two other exceedingly important
interests. One is the Jewish people; the other, the world.*

—Charles Ryrie

In the months after the 9/11 tragedy, I saw more flag waving and heard more renditions of "God Bless America" than throughout the rest of my life combined. The incredible outpouring of patriotism and unity in America was refreshing to see.

Yet as we find our world marching toward the final years of this age, one question we should all want answered is this: Can we do anything to move the heart of God to continue to bless our nation? What can we do as a nation and as individuals to ensure the continued favor of God upon us as a people?

The answer is really quite simple: we can continue to experience God's favor as a nation by following God's prescription for national blessing. Three main keys to national blessing are set forth in Scripture. Two of these are what we might call God's "foreign policy," and one is His "domestic policy." We would be wise as a nation and in our individual lives to continue to follow these three guidelines.

Friends of Israel

The first biblical key to national blessing and God's foreign policy is blessing the Jewish people. All the way back in Genesis 12:3, God made an amazing promise to Abraham and his descendants that has never been revoked. "And I will bless those who bless you, and the one who curses you I will curse." Literally, we could translate this, "Those who bless you I will bless, and the one who curses you I *must* curse." This is God's only "direct" foreign policy statement in all the Bible. Those who support the Jewish people will be blessed and those who curse them must be cursed.

This ancient promise from God has never been repealed or abrogated. It still stands today. And throughout history we have seen both its blessings and its curses played out on the stage of human history. Someone has joked that, ironically, every time someone tries to wipe out the Jewish people, they end up with a new holiday. The Jewish Passover feast arose from Pharaoh's ill-fated attempt to destroy the firstborn Jewish males. Hamaan's wicked plot to destroy the Jews resulted in the establishment of the feast of Purim, as recounted in the book of Esther. The hatred of the Syrian king Antiochus Epiphanes for the Jews and his blasphemous defiling of the Jewish temple inspired the Jewish feast of Hanukkah, or the Festival of Lights. While Hitler's Holocaust didn't result in a Jewish holiday, God's retribution against Israel's oppressors was on full display for the world to see.

Charles Ryrie observes, "The Jewish people…are the apple of God's eye (Zechariah 2:8).… The friends and enemies of Abraham and his progeny are the friends and enemies of God. History has verified this principle."[1]

The United States was the first country to recognize the State of Israel.

Throughout Israel's tumultuous, turbulent history, the United States has consistently been its close ally and supporter. American support for Israel today is more important than ever. Israel's problems, threats, and challenges are much more complicated and deadly than in the past, and at the same time, standing with Israel is becoming much more unpopular. An anti-Israel, anti-U.S. attitude pervades the United Nations.[2] Add to that the jihadist hatred for Israel. America is under growing pressure to "throw Israel under the bus." Fortunately, America's resolve to back the Jewish state remains fairly solid.

According to a survey taken in April 2008 of a thousand American Christians, there is still overwhelming support for Israel. This is very good news. It's a key line of defense for our nation. Among the results of the poll, "more than 80 percent of American Christians say they have a 'moral and biblical obligation' to support the State of Israel, and half say Jerusalem should remain its undivided capital." In fact, the data shows that all the large American Christian denominations, including a large portion of Catholics, carry strong pro-Israel convictions.[3]

These statistics reflect what we've seen throughout America's history: America has consistently remained Israel's chief ally. We have committed many grievous sins as a nation, but we've continued as a steadfast friend of the Jews and the nation of Israel.

America today surpasses all other nations in our support for Israel. Our economic and military aid each year totals somewhere in the neighborhood of $3–4 billion, depending on which statistics you use. Since 1973, according to the *Christian Science Monitor*, Israel has cost the United States about $1.6 trillion. If you divide that by today's population, it comes out to more than $5,700 per person.[4] About 12 percent of American foreign aid goes to Israel, which is a total of about 2.5 billion USD per year. American aid makes up 7–8 percent of the total Israeli national budget.[5]

The situation is clear—unless things change dramatically, without the United States, Israel would be incinerated in a matter of days by its hostile Arab neighbors and their allies. Since Israel is pictured in Scripture as a thriving nation in the end times, barring any radical changes, I believe America must remain strong until the time of the Rapture to serve as Israel's chief ally and protector.

Might we continue even longer in God's blessing if we continue to bless the offspring of Abraham?

The New Anti-Semitism

Anti-Semitism is nothing new. It's been around ever since God promised that the Messiah would come through the line of Abraham, Isaac, and Jacob. Satan tried to keep Jesus from being born, tried to kill Him *after* He was born, and has worked since Jesus ascended back to heaven to keep the Jewish people from being regathered to their land in fulfillment of God's promises. The devil wants to thwart the promises of God. He also knows that the Jewish people are God's timepiece and that their national conversion will trigger the Second Coming of Christ and spell his doom. So it's no wonder the Jewish people have been subjected to endless persecution and countless pogroms throughout their history. However, recent times have seen a novel variation on the theme, often dubbed "the new anti-Semitism." So how is it different?

Simply stated, the new anti-Semitism is now focused on the modern State of Israel. It's more subtle than the older form—not hatred directed toward the Jewish people per se but a fervor directed at national Israel and anything they stand for. The new anti-Semitism is anti-Israelism, or anti-Zionism. Even though Israel is the only functioning democracy in the region, anti-Israel sentiment is often justified by appealing to alleged Israeli atrocities and the plight of Palestinians. Anti-Israel demonstrations are becoming more commonplace on college campuses, and demonstrators even compare Israel with Nazi Germany.

The new anti-Semitism, led by radical jihadists, wants the destruction of Israel and everyone in it. Part of the mix is a growing Western indifference as radical Islam's hatred for Israel becomes the "new normal." But in reality, this "new" hostility is nothing more than the old anti-Semitism in new clothes. America, led by Christians, must stand against the new anti-Semitism and with the State of Israel if the United States is to enjoy the blessings promised in the Abrahamic covenant in Genesis 12:3.

The Danger of Replacement Theology

Sadly, a growing number of American Christians favor weakening or even abandoning support for Israel. Some of the impetus behind this comes from those who have adopted an errant view that the nation of Israel no longer has any special significance to God and has no special role to play in the unfolding drama of the ages. This view often includes the idea that national Israel has been permanently replaced by the church.

Historically, this is called "replacement theology"—that is, "the view that the church is the new or true Israel that has permanently replaced or superseded Israel as the people of God."[6] Another term, often found in academic circles, is the older term "supersessionism" (the belief that the church has *superseded* Israel).[7] Replacement theology has been the fuel within Christendom that energized medieval anti-Semitism, Eastern European pogroms, the Holocaust, and contemporary disdain for the modern State of Israel. Michael J. Vlach notes, "The acceptance or rejection of supersessionism may also influence how one views the modern State of Israel and events in the Middle East."[8] As my friend Thomas Ice has said, "Wherever replacement theology has flourished, the Jews have had to run for cover."

Ronald Diprose notes that an early form of replacement theology began in the second century with Justin Martyr, and describes it as the belief that "Israel has been repudiated by God and has been replaced by the Church in the working out of his plan. A variation of this idea is that true Israel always has been the Church."[9] I agree that the New Testament often affirms Christ's fulfillment of the Old Testament, but nowhere does the Bible indicate that Old Testament promises to ethnic Israel are fulfilled in the church. I don't believe there's a single passage in the entire New Testament where language that speaks of Israel or the Jews is used to directly refer to anyone who is not ethnically Israel.

Hebrew Christian Arnold G. Fruchtenbaum, in his PhD dissertation,[10] has studied every use of Israel in the New Testament[11] and says, "The conclusion is that the Church is never called, and is not, a 'spiritual Israel' or a 'new Israel.' The term *Israel* is either used of the nation or the people as a whole, or of the believing remnant within. It is never used of the Church in general or of Gentile believers in particular."[12] New Testament scholar Robert L. Thomas says, "No clear cut example of the church being called 'Israel' exists in the NT or in ancient church writings until AD 160."[13] So it was well after the final book of the New Testament was written, after the apostolic era, that such a view was first suggested. I believe that replacement theology is the result of a failure to interpret the Bible according to a consistently literal or natural method of interpretation.

Modern Israel's Right to the Land

All throughout the Old Testament, God says that the land we know as Israel is for the descendants of Abraham, Isaac, and Jacob—that is, the Jews. Every Old Testament prophet, except Jonah and Nahum, speaks of a permanent return to the land of Israel by the Jews.[14] Nowhere in the New Testament are these Old Testament promises ever changed or negated.[15] In fact, they are reinforced by some New Testament passages (Matthew 19:28; Acts 1:6; Romans 11:1–2). The apostle Paul says that Israel today is "beloved" by God on account of the original, irrevocable promise made to Abraham, Isaac, and Jacob (Romans 11:28). Paul declares the promises to Israel: "The gifts and the calling of God are irrevocable" (verse 29).[16]

The only legitimate basis for the Jews to claim a right to the land of Israel comes from God and the Bible. In fact, if it were not for the biblical history of Israel, who would even know to associate the Jewish people with the land of Israel? It is precisely because God gave them their land—located in today's Middle East—and makes this link that we can even have a movement today known as Zionism.

The Lord called Abram out of Ur of the Chaldeans and made an unconditional covenant, or contract, with him. This contract, known as the Abrahamic covenant, contained three major provisions: (1) a land to Abram and his descendants, (2) a "seed" or physical descendants of Abraham, and (3) a worldwide blessing (Genesis 12:1–3).

In order to make it clear that His promise was unconditional, the Lord put Abram to sleep and made Himself the only signer of the contract (Genesis 15:1–21). God told Abram, "To your descendants I have given this land" (verse 18). Even though the Lord sealed the covenant unilaterally and unconditionally, nevertheless it is clear that Abraham obeyed the Lord during his lifetime: "Abraham obeyed Me and kept My charge, My commandments, My statutes and My laws" (Genesis 26:5). This covenant was reiterated to Abraham, Isaac, and Jacob and their descendants about twenty times in the book of Genesis.[17] God's promise to the patriarchs was repeatedly described as an everlasting covenant (Genesis 17:7, 13, 19).

Abraham had two sons, Ishmael (father of the Arab nations) and Isaac (father of Israel). By specific revelation, God passed the covenant promise of the land of Abraham to Isaac, instead of Ishmael. The Lord told Isaac: "Sojourn in this land and I will be with you and bless you, for to you and to your descendants I will give all these lands, and I will establish the oath which I swore to your father Abraham. I will multiply your descendants as the stars of heaven, and will give your descendants all these lands; and by your descendants all the nations of the earth shall be blessed" (Genesis 26:3–4). The same promise God had made to the father (see Genesis 12:3; 15:18), He repeated to the chosen son, Isaac.

Isaac also produced two sons, the twins Jacob and Esau. From this third generation, God identified Jacob (and his descendants) as the recipient of the covenant promises, rather than Esau (father of the Edomites). God later changed Jacob's name to Israel, which became the primary name of the new nation. In Jacob's famous dream of a stairway from heaven to earth, the Lord said, "I am the LORD, the God of your father Abraham and the God of Isaac; the land on which you lie, I will give it to you and to your descendants. Your descendants will also be like the dust of the earth, and you will spread out to the west and to the east and to the north and to the south; and in you and in your descendants shall all the families of the earth be blessed" (Genesis 28:13–14). Notice in this statement the repetition of all three components from God's covenant with Abraham: worldwide blessing, offspring…and the land. By divine decree, claim to the Promised Land passed through Abraham and Isaac to Jacob's posterity—his twelve sons, the fathers of Israel's twelve tribes.

Genesis closes with Jacob, his twelve sons, and their descendants sojourning in the land of Egypt. Exodus is the story of their deliverance from Egypt and preparation for entrance into the Promised Land, then known as Canaan. While Israel wandered in the wilderness for forty years because of unbelief, Moses received the Law that would become the new nation's constitution, by which it would be governed in the land.

The book of Deuteronomy repeats at least twenty-five times that the land is a gift to the people of Israel from the Lord (for example, Deuteronomy 1:20, 25; 2:29; 3:20; 4:40; 5:16).

Before, during, and after the exile of many Jews from their homeland, the Old Testament prophets, God's spokesmen to humanity, affirmed promise after promise of Israel's future restoration to the land (Isaiah 11:1–9; 12:1–3; 27:12–13; 35:1–10; 43:1–8; 60:18–21; 66:20–22; Jeremiah 16:14–16; 30:10–18; 31:31–37; 32:37–40; Ezekiel 11:17–21; 28:25–26; 34:11–16; 37:21–25; 39:25–29; Hosea 1:10–11; 3:4–5; Joel 3:17–21; Amos 9:11–15; Micah 4:4–7; Zephaniah 3:14–20; Zechariah 8:4–8; 10:1–12).

It's important to note that Zechariah lived and prophesied *after* the Jews' return to their homeland from captivity. And yet God, through Zechariah, speaks of a future restoration to the land, thus suggesting that Israel's past restorations did not ultimately fulfill the land promise given to Abraham, Isaac, and Jacob. Zechariah 9–14 lays out an end-time plan of restoration of the nation to Jerusalem and the Promised Land.

The Jewish people are the only ethnic group in history to whom God has promised a particular piece of real estate on this earth. God has given them the title deed to the land of Israel. He promised the land to Abraham and his descendants, through Isaac and Jacob, forever. Israel has a future in this land, because nowhere in the Bible has the Lord specifically revoked any of His promises to His people Israel. "For the gifts and the calling of God are irrevocable" (Romans 11:29).

America and Modern Israel

With that brief overview of Israel's place in the Bible and history, we can see that God still has a future for Israel and the Jewish people. We can also see that the promise of curses and blessings from Genesis 12:3 is still in effect today. Those who argue that the modern State of Israel has no biblical significance are in error, in my opinion. While America isn't mentioned specifically in the Bible, one could argue that America's support for Israel has brought us into the eye of the prophetic hurricane. So far, America has received good grades on God's report card in dealing with the Jewish people. Anti-Semitism has never taken firm root on American soil. Jews have fared well in this land. I pray that it remains that way, because I love this country and the Jewish people. Charles Dyer states the issue forcefully: "The minute the United States turns its back on the State of Israel, we have made ourselves the enemy of God."[18]

Of course, this doesn't mean that as individuals or as a nation Americans have to agree with or condone everything that Israel does. Some of the decisions the Israeli government makes are unjust and should be opposed.

Charles Ryrie wisely says, "People, not politics, are God's chief concern and the Jewish people, not Israeli politics, should be the Christian's interest."[19] However, as individuals and as a nation we must never adopt an anti-Semitic stance or place ourselves in a position that is actively hostile to the Jewish people or even be satisfied with a neutral stance. We must never cease to be pro-Israel and affirm Israel's right to exist as a nation in the land God has promised it.

Rather, we should continue to look for ways to bless the Jews and their nation. As Ryrie concludes, "In the meanwhile, let America remember that a great nation is marked by her kind treatment of the Jewish people. God keeps His promises, and He will bless those who are friendly toward the 'friend of God' and his descendants."[20]

What About the Future?

There's no disputing the fact that America has been a friend to the Jewish people and that God has blessed this action. But what about the future? Will U.S. support of Israel continue in the face of mounting threats by radical Islamists? What will happen to U.S. support for Israel after the Rapture? After the Rapture occurs and all the true believers are removed from the U.S. population, I wouldn't be surprised if America begins to turn against Israel. After all, evangelical Christians are the vanguard of support for the Jewish people and the modern State of Israel. Once all believers are removed, a new, even more virulent strain of anti-Semitism could easily erupt. As America faces the ongoing malice of Muslim extremism and growing pressure from the Far Left, the chant to end support for Israel will grow louder and will become much more likely to succeed after the Rapture. Withdrawal of support for Israel would bring God's judgment and could be a further cause of the demise of America as a leading nation in the end times.

The Beautiful People

While God has a keen interest in the Jewish people, it's important for us to understand that He is the God of the nations. He cares about the salvation of all people. For this reason, the second biblical key to national blessing (God's foreign policy) is faithfully sharing the good news (the gospel) of salvation with a needy world. This is the good news: God made the ultimate sacrifice by sending His Son, Jesus, to die on the cross in the place of sinful people, paying the penalty for our sins, and He rose again on the third day.

Romans 10:15 reveals the heart of God toward those who take His precious gospel to the lost: "How beautiful are the feet of those who bring good news of good things!" We don't often think of feet as the most attractive part of our bodies, but God says that feet that spread the Good News are indeed beautiful. Those who take part in spreading the Good News to a needy world are beautiful in the sight of God.

I believe a key ingredient in God's blessing on America is its active promotion and support of the gospel around the globe. God has been merciful to the United States simply because so many people have financed missions and have personally taken the good news of the gospel to others in this world. No other nation's faithfulness in this respect even comes close to America's. This is beautiful to God, and He blesses it.

In a nutshell, that's God's foreign policy for nations today: bless Israel and spread the good news to the nations. But what is His domestic policy for maintaining His hand of blessing upon our nation?

Righteousness Exalts a Nation

The third and final way we can invoke the blessing of God upon our nation is by practicing justice and righteousness in our own lives and promoting righteousness in the society at large. This is God's domestic policy for nations. We need to be reminded that the fate of a nation is not ultimately dependent upon politics, military might, or economics, but on righteousness, goodness, and mercy.

Psalm 33:12 says, "Blessed is the nation whose God is the LORD." Proverbs 14:34 is crystal clear: "Righteousness exalts a nation, but sin is a disgrace to any people." Psalm 9:17 states the promise negatively: "The wicked will return to Sheol, even all the nations who forget God."

One important way we can ensure the continued outpouring of God's blessing is to elect godly leaders, to pray for them (1 Timothy 2:2), to support and vote for government policies that are righteous and good, to speak out and vote against government policies and actions that are unrighteous and harmful, and to practice personal holiness in our own lives. That's God's domestic policy for every nation, and those who follow it will be blessed.

Let's Get Personal

Let's review: The Bible contains no specific prophetic mentions of America. The most logical conclusion is that America will end up as a part of the Antichrist's Western coalition after the Rapture. However, in the meantime we must never forget three simple, yet important, lessons for our nation: be good to the Jewish people and Israel; be actively involved in the spread of the gospel of salvation to the whole world; and do all you can to practice and promote righteousness in your neighborhood, city, state, and our nation at large.

This will please the Father and continue His blessing upon America.

Now, as important as it is for you to know all of this big-picture stuff, it's much more important that you know what's going to happen to *you* when it all comes down or when you die, whichever comes first. But how can you know? (How can *I* know?)

Is there any sure word about *your* future?

11

NO FEAR
OF THE
STORM

He who believes in the Son has eternal life. (John 3:36)

I am the resurrection and the life; he who believes in Me will live even if he dies. (John 11:25)

I am the way, and the truth, and the life; no one comes to the Father but through Me. (John 14:6)
—Jesus Christ

Talk about the future and the end times can be frightening for some people. Many view it as a purely negative, hopelessly depressing doomsday scenario that's unsettling, even scary. Maybe you feel like that sometimes. But you don't have to. According to the Bible, you can know for sure what will happen to *you* when you leave this earth. You don't need to be afraid of death or the future.

Let me ask you a very simple, very personal question: Are you ready for the coming of the Lord Jesus? Would you be left behind if the Rapture happened today? Do you know for sure where you stand with the Lord?

You can be prepared for the Rapture or your death, whichever comes first, by trusting Jesus Christ as your personal Savior from sin. The Bible calls this being "born again" (John 3:7), or being "saved" (Acts 4:12). In His mercy, God has made salvation from sin and judgment very simple. In fact, it is so simple that many people stumble over the simplicity. God says that we must become like children and be "converted" to enter heaven (Matthew 18:1–3).

There are three basic things a person must believe and accept to have his sins forgiven. First, you must recognize that you are a sinner—that is, that you have sinned against a holy God by breaking His laws and commandments. Romans 3:23 says that we have all sinned and come short of the glory of God. Just think, it took only one sin for Adam and Eve to be excluded from the Garden of Eden forever, and it only takes one sin to keep any of the rest of us out of heaven forever.

Second, you must admit that you need a Savior. No matter how much good you may have done in your life, you cannot get rid of your sins. You cannot save yourself. You need a Savior, a Rescuer (Titus 3:5–6).

Third, you must believe that Jesus Christ is that Savior you need, who died for you on the cross and rose again. And you must receive and accept Him by faith (John 1:12–13). There are no magical words or particular prayers that will bring salvation, but the following sample prayer can serve as a guide if you want to turn to Christ right now. If you truly mean these words as you pray them, you will receive eternal life right where you are (John 3:36).

> Lord, I admit that I am a sinner. I have gone my own way in life and have broken Your laws and commands. I recognize that I cannot save myself by my own good works. I must have a Savior. And I believe that Jesus Christ is the Savior who died for me on the cross and rose again. I receive Him now by faith, trusting in Him alone for complete forgiveness and salvation from sin.

Don't Put It Off Any Longer

Pray this prayer right now and receive Jesus Christ as your Savior and Lord. Be prepared for the future. God promises in His Word that "whoever will call on the name of the Lord will be saved" (Romans 10:13). Call on Him in faith right now! Put your hand in His hand like a little child, and trust Him with your eternal salvation. It's the best decision you will ever make. You will have no reason to ever fear the future again.

Don't wait! The Rapture may come at any moment.

Don't be left behind!

Be ready.

SOME QUESTIONS
YOU MIGHT
BE ASKING

Discussion of end-time prophecy always raises many questions, especially when considering any role that America might play. I hope reading this book has answered some of your questions. But I'm sure it has raised some others. Here are a few of the most-asked questions that I commonly hear relating to America in the end times. I hope these answers help you understand this subject more thoroughly.

Question #1: Is it legitimate for American Christians to rely on 2 Chronicles 7:14 for national blessing?

American Christians today commonly refer to 2 Chronicles 7:14 and apply it to our nation. The passage says, "[If] My people who are called by My name humble themselves and pray and seek My face and turn from their wicked ways, then I will hear from heaven, will forgive their sin and will heal their land." This is a great verse that contains a powerful promise of hope and restoration. But is it for America? As with any biblical text, the key to proper interpretation and understanding is to put it into its original setting and context.

Second Chronicles 7:14 is God's word to King Solomon of Israel at the dedication of the temple in Jerusalem. God promises that when the people of

Israel are under divine discipline for disobedience and they humbly call upon Him, He will hear and heal their land.

From the context it is clear that "My people" refers to Israel and "their land" refers to the land of Israel. This verse is basically a summary reiteration of the conditions for national blessing, previously set forth in God's covenant with Israel in Deuteronomy 28.

In 2 Chronicles 7:15, the Lord continues by saying, "Now My eyes will be open and My ears attentive to the prayer offered in this place." The place where the prayer is offered is the temple in Jerusalem. Obviously, believers in America are not the nation of Israel, our land is not the Promised Land in Israel, and we don't offer prayers for our nation from the temple mount in Jerusalem. This promise was a direct promise to the nation of Israel at the dedication of the temple in Jerusalem. For these reasons, I do not believe it is legitimate for believers today to *directly* claim 2 Chronicles 7:14 as a promise of national revival and restoration in America.

However, having said that, I do see clear principles in this verse that we can and should apply to our own lives today. We do this all the time with Old Testament scriptures that don't directly address our situation. After we interpret the passage and discover its meaning in its context, we then look for the timeless truth in the passage that God would have us apply to our lives. After all, the Bible tells us that "all Scripture is inspired by God and profitable for teaching, for reproof, for correction, for training in righteousness; so that the man of God may be adequate, equipped for every good work" (2 Timothy 3:16–17).

I believe the timeless truth for us to apply from 2 Chronicles 7:14 is that God desires obedience and humility in His people and that when we come to Him in that way, He hears our cry and brings blessing. This implies seeking a personal, face-to-face relationship with Him and living in obedience to His Word. If we will faithfully do this, we can be assured that God will bless us and, through us, our community and nation.

Question #2: Will U.S. political efforts successfully bring peace to the Middle East?

Ever since I can remember, there has been turmoil in the Middle East, and Israel has been in the eye of the hurricane. The Six Days' War in 1967. The Yom Kippur War in 1973. The war with Lebanon in 1982. The intifada of 2001. The thirty-four-day Second Lebanon War with Hamas and Hezbollah in the summer of 2006.

Peace in the Middle East is the most pursued, treasured prize in international diplomacy—and the most elusive. Administration after American administration has each taken their crack at resolving the ongoing conflict and, at its heart, the chronic, thorny Israeli-Palestinian mess.

The genesis of the modern Middle East peace process really began about ninety years ago. The two main parties in this effort were Emir Feisal, the son of the sherif of Mecca and Medina, and Chaim Weizmann, the leader of world Zionism, who later became the first president of Israel. These men did forge an agreement in 1918, but it never got off the ground because of a lack of French and British support.

More recently, the peace process has been plowing uphill for about sixty years. The official foundation of Israel as a nation on May 14, 1948, initiated one long peace process between Israel and its Arab neighbors. But, alas, no peace. Only brief periods of no war.

The Arab nations surrounding Israel have existed in a declared state of war with Israel since its 1948 independence day. Here is a brief sketch of the hostilities to date between Israel and its neighbors.

1948–49—*The formation of Israel.* When Israel officially became an independent state on May 14, 1948, it was immediately attacked from all sides by Egypt, Jordan, Iraq, Syria, Lebanon, and Saudi Arabia. By the time a truce was implemented on January 7, 1949, Israel had expanded its territory from five thousand square miles to eight thousand, including much of the Negev, the huge desert to the south, between Israel and Egypt.

1956—*The Suez War between Egypt and Israel.* Egyptian leader Gamal Abdel Nasser nationalized the Suez Canal. On October 29, 1956, Israel invaded the Sinai Peninsula and took control. Later, Israel returned the Sinai to Egypt.

1964—*The formation of the Palestinian Liberation Organization (PLO).* It was formed with the dual purpose of creating a Palestinian State and destroying Israel.

1967—*The famous Six Days' War (June 5–10).* Israel captured the Sinai Peninsula from Egypt, the West Bank from Jordan, and the Golan Heights from Syria, and seized control of Jerusalem.

1973—*The Yom Kippur War.* At 2:00 p.m. on October 6, 1973, on Israel's most holy day, the Day of Atonement (Yom Kippur), Israel was attacked by Egypt and Syria. After heavy fighting, Israel repelled the invaders.

1982–85—*The War with Lebanon.*

1987—*The first Palestinian intifada (uprising) in Gaza.* This uprising ended in 1993 with the signing of the Oslo Accords.

2000—*The second Palestinian intifada.* In this uprising, which began in September 2000, the Palestinians employed suicide (homicide) bombers.

2006—*Open war between Israel and Hamas and Hezbollah.*

As you can see, the brief history of modern Israel is a history of war, sprinkled liberally with futile attempts to grab the phantom of peace.

In the United States, president after president, secretary of state after secretary of state have failed to make any real, lasting headway in the ongoing hostilities between Israel and its neighbors. The United States was able to broker peace treaties between Israel and Egypt and Jordan. But both of these nations continue to harbor deep hatred toward Israel and consistently side with other Arab nations in political conflicts. The Oslo Accords, signed on September 13, 1993, on the White House lawn by Yitzhak Rabin and Yasir Arafat, brought great hope. But the second intifada, which began on September 26, 2000, between Israel and the Palestinians, dashed any hopes that the Oslo Accords had raised. The Roadmap to Peace, which was formulated in 2003 by the United States, the European Union, the United Nations, and Russia, and which proposes a two-state solution, is the most recent strategy for forging a Middle East peace.

But try as they may, no diplomat, secretary, or president will be able to bring lasting peace to the Middle East. The Bible says peace will come to the Middle East only when the Lord Jesus sets His feet back on this earth to rule and reign. However, before the true Christ returns to bring real peace, the false Christ will establish a counterfeit kingdom and bring a three-and-a-half-year pseudopeace to Israel. The first clue in Scripture as to the identity of the Antichrist is found in Daniel 9:27, where he is pictured brokering a treaty with Israel: "And he [Antichrist] will make a firm covenant with the many for one week [seven years]." This means that when the world gets its first glimpse of the Antichrist, he will appear as a great peacemaker.

What is the exact nature of this covenant that the Antichrist will make with Israel? Charles H. Dyer answers:

> Daniel does not specify its content, but he does indicate that it will extend for seven years. During the first half of this time Israel feels at peace and secure, so the covenant must provide some guarantee for Israel's national security. Very likely the covenant will allow Israel to be at peace with her Arab neighbors. One result of the covenant is that Israel will be allowed to rebuild her temple in Jerusalem. This world ruler will succeed where [Henry] Kissinger, [Jimmy] Carter, [Ronald] Reagan, [George H. W.] Bush, and other world leaders have failed. He will be known as the man of peace![1]

It's interesting that in recent years the Arabs and Israelis are looking more and more to Europe as the mediator to bring peace to the region. This is exactly what the Bible predicts in Daniel 9:27.

After the Antichrist—the leader of Europe—brokers his peace deal, all will go along just fine until the midpoint of the seven years. That's when the Antichrist will break his treaty with Israel, invade the land, desecrate the rebuilt temple in Jerusalem by setting up an image of himself in the holy of holies, and proclaim himself god. This event will touch off the final three and a half years of this age, called by Jesus the "great tribulation" (Matthew 24:21).

The world will then endure a time of horror unlike any it has ever known. The only hope for peace in the Middle East and the entire world will be the Prince of Peace, the Lord Jesus Christ, who will return in great power and glory to subdue His enemies and inaugurate His worldwide kingdom. Then, and only then, will peace come to the Middle East and the rest of the world.

However, the impossibility of lasting peace in the Middle East until Christ comes should not deter us from doing all we can as a people and a nation to stop further bloodshed in that region. We should support and pray for our government leaders as they do the best they can to bring some resolution to the problems in *every* part of the world that suffers violence, bloodshed, and conflict. Remember the words of Jesus: "Blessed are the peacemakers" (Matthew 5:9).

Question #3: Could the Antichrist come from the United States?

According to Scripture, the coming Antichrist will be a Gentile who will rule the entire world for three and a half years. Since America is the most powerful nation in the world, people often ask if the Antichrist could come from the United States or even if he could be a U.S. president, an individual holding the most powerful office on earth.

Daniel 9:26 tells us that the Antichrist will be of the same nationality as the people who destroyed the Jewish temple in AD 70. Of course, we know that the Romans destroyed the temple. Therefore, we know that the Antichrist will be of Roman origin—that is, he will rise out of the reunited Roman Empire.

Interestingly, the 1976 classic film *The Omen* begins with the birth of the Antichrist in a dimly lit hospital in Rome. A chilling poem from this same movie reinforces the belief that the coming Antichrist will arise from the revived Roman Empire.

> When the Jews return to Zion
> And a comet rips the sky
> And the Holy Roman Empire rises,
> Then you and I must die.
>
> From the eternal sea he rises,
> Creating armies on either shore,
> Turning man against his brother
> Till man exists no more.

As we look at our world today, the Jews have returned to Zion and the reunited Roman Empire is rising before our eyes in the European Union. The rise of the Antichrist may not be far behind!

The "Roman Empire" limits the Antichrist's place of origin to Europe, the Middle East, or North Africa. Most people have taken this to mean that he will come out of one of the nations of Europe that formed the nucleus of the old Roman Empire, possibly even Rome itself. However, since the United States came from European nations that constituted the Roman Empire and has language and laws derived from Rome, is it possible that the Antichrist could come from America? Could he even be an American president?

No one can say for sure. While it's possible he could be an American, it seems most likely that the Antichrist will come out of Europe. This was the Roman Empire that existed in John's day, when he prophesied the Antichrist's coming from a future form of that empire. However, regardless of his specific origin, one thing is sure: he is coming. And he will do exactly what the Bible predicts.

Question #4: Is America really a nation "under God"?

Every morning in school for thirteen years of their lives, the first thing American children do is recite the Pledge of Allegiance to the American flag and all that it represents. In this pledge they boldly declare that the United States is "one nation under God." The original pledge was composed on September 8, 1892, to commemorate the four hundredth anniversary of Columbus's discovery of America. The pledge underwent subsequent revisions in 1923 and 1924 and was made official by Congress in 1942. It was given the official title "The Pledge of Allegiance" in 1945. The last change to the pledge occurred on July 14 (Flag Day), 1954, when President Dwight D. Eisenhower approved the addition of the words "under God." While authorizing the change, Eisenhower said, "In this way we are reaffirming the transcendence of religious faith in America's heritage and future; in this way we shall constantly strengthen those spiritual weapons which forever will be our country's most powerful resource in peace and war."[2]

These words have come under heated assault by atheists and other secularists who are making concerted efforts to get them eliminated from the pledge.

While this wonderful phrase is unique to our nation's pledge, it could really be incorporated into the pledge of any nation because all nations are under God. Most people fail to recognize this fact, but the truth still remains—all the nations of the earth and their leaders are under the sovereign hand of God, whether they believe it or not. This applies even to those in America who want to remove every vestige of the words "under God" from our national consciousness. Theirs is the height of denial.

Very early in the pages of the Bible, Scripture makes abundantly clear that all nations are under God.

When the Most High gave the nations their inheritance,
When He separated the sons of man,
He set the boundaries of the peoples
According to the number of the sons of Israel. (Deuteronomy 32:8)

He makes the nations great, then destroys them;
He enlarges the nations, then leads them away. (Job 12:23)

King David, the greatest ruler of Israel, acknowledged the rule of God over all the heavens and earth:

Blessed are You, O LORD God of Israel our father, forever and ever.
Yours, O LORD is the greatness and the power and the glory and the victory and the majesty, indeed everything that is in the heavens and the earth; Yours is the dominion, O LORD, and You exalt Yourself as head over all. Both riches and honor come from You, and You rule over all, and in Your hand is power and might; and it lies in Your hand to make great and strengthen everyone.
(1 Chronicles 29:10–12)

In the book of Daniel, God reminded the great king of Babylon, Nebuchadnezzar, that He rules over man's kingdoms:

Let the name of God be blessed forever and ever,
For wisdom and power belong to Him.
It is He who changes the times and the epochs;
He removes kings and establishes kings;
He gives wisdom to wise men
And knowledge to men of understanding.
(Daniel 2:20–21)

In order that the living may know
That the Most High is ruler over the realm of mankind,
And bestows it on whom He wishes
And sets over it the lowliest of men. (Daniel 4:17)

For His dominion is an everlasting dominion,
And His kingdom endures from generation to generation.
All the inhabitants of the earth are accounted as nothing,
But He does according to His will in the host of heaven
And among the inhabitants of earth;
And no one can ward off His hand
Or say to Him, "What have You done?" (Daniel 4:34–35)

Later, in the first century AD, the apostle Paul reminded the inhabitants of the mighty city of Athens that all the nations of the earth are "under God." During his second missionary journey, Paul arrived in Athens and was overcome by the idolatry in the city. On Mars Hill he addressed the council of philosophers and reminded them of the most important truth for any group of people to understand—that God is the Creator of all things and that He has already determined the course of every nation. "He is the God who made the world and everything in it…. He himself gives life and breath to everything, and he satisfies every need. From one man he created all the nations throughout the whole earth. He decided beforehand when they should rise and fall, and he determined their boundaries" (Acts 17:24–26, NLT).

Paul even clarified God's reason for this: "His purpose was for the nations to seek after God and perhaps feel their way toward him and find him—though he is not far from any one of us. For in him we live and move and exist" (Acts 17:27–28, NLT).

Can you imagine preaching this message to Alexander the Great, Napoleon, Hitler, Saddam Hussein, or to many in affluent America? Can you fathom telling them that the God of heaven has already determined the limits of their expansion, the extent and importance of their influence in the world, and the duration of their existence in world affairs? Yet it's true. God is sovereign over the lives of individuals and of nations. He is Lord of all.

Ray Stedman, the noted pastor and author, once traveled to England to speak at a Bible conference. The sanctuary of the church was filled with people who came to hear this well-known Bible teacher. The service began with a time of singing and praise to the Lord. One of the songs the people sang was the now popular—but then unknown—chorus, "Our God Reigns."

Stedman was seated on the platform next to the pastor of the church, singing with the congregation. As he glanced down at the song sheet, he began to smile. Then laugh.

Why was he laughing? The words on the song sheet had been mistyped. Instead of singing, "Our God Reigns," the congregation was singing, at the top of their lungs, "Our God Resigns."[3]

This story is funny, but how often do we do the same thing? While we have never sung those erroneous words, how often do we look at the world around us and wonder if God has resigned and is no longer seated on His throne in heaven, ruling the nations. We need to remind ourselves that God remains enthroned in heaven and continues to reign over all. Including America. The secularists in our nation need to be reminded of this sobering fact. And so do many professing Christians. We may mouth the words "one nation under God," but do we truly believe it and live as though it's true? There is often a wide gap between what we profess to believe in theory and our actual practice and mind-set.

We must actively exert whatever influence we have to move our public policy toward doing good, loving mercy, and promoting righteousness. Are we adopting national policies that reflect our awareness that God reigns over all and that we are ultimately accountable to Him? *Saying* we are "under God" and *believing and living* it are two different things.

Question #5: Will troops from the United States be at Armageddon?

We can confidently say that the United States will participate in Armageddon. Two main points support this conclusion. First, this confidence arises from the fact that Scripture indicates that all the nations of the world will be gathered against Israel at Armageddon.

> Zechariah 12:3: "It will come about in that day that I will make Jerusalem a heavy stone for all the peoples; all who lift it will be severely injured. And *all the nations of the earth* will be gathered against it."

> Zechariah 14:2: "For I will gather *all the nations* against Jerusalem to battle, and the city will be captured, the houses plundered, the women ravished and half of the city exiled, but the rest of the people will not be cut off from the city."

> Revelation 16:14: "For they are spirits of demons, performing signs, which go out to *the kings of the whole world,* to gather them together for the war of the great day of God, the Almighty."

This does not mean that every nation currently in existence will be at Armageddon, since the political face of the world may change drastically between now and then. However, it does mean that the United States, in whatever form it takes at that time, will invade Israel with all the rest of the world at Armageddon.

The second reason I believe American troops will participate in Armageddon is that we know that the Antichrist will lead the West in their invasion of Israel at the end of the Tribulation. Since I have concluded that America will be part of the Antichrist's Western empire in the end times, it follows that America will be a part of the events of Armageddon. Today,

America is Israel's chief ally and protector. But in the end times even America will follow the Antichrist in turning against Israel and the Jewish people. No doubt America's abandonment of Israel after the Rapture will play a large part in its demise.

Appendix B

COME LEARN FROM MY MENTORS

In any age, but particularly in our own, it's important to keep in touch with the past. Far too often in our fast-paced, forward-looking culture, we fail to take time to look back and listen to some of the giants of the faith from past generations. This is unfortunate. And I hope to help correct this in my books.

The book excerpts in this appendix are adapted from two men whom I have met, whom I highly respect, and from whom I have learned a great deal—Dr. John F. Walvoord and Dr. Tim LaHaye.[1] As you may have noticed, I quoted both of these men several times in this book.

I've included these excerpts so you can see that my basic views have been held by other respected scholars and Bible teachers and because much of my thinking on this subject has been shaped by them. I hope you enjoy them as much as I have.

From *The Nations in Prophecy,* by Dr. John F. Walvoord, 1967

One of the natural questions facing the world, but especially citizens of the United States of America, is the place of the United States in the unfulfilled prophetic program. In the last fifty years, the United States of America has become one of the most powerful and influential nations of all history. What does the Bible contribute to the question of the future of the United States?

In keeping with the principle that prophecy is primarily concerned with the Holy Land and its immediate neighbors, it is not surprising that geographic areas remote from this center of Biblical interest should not figure largely in prophecy and may not be mentioned at all. No specific mention of the United States or any other country in North America or South America can be found in the Bible. None of the rather obscure references to distant lands can be taken specifically as a reference to the United States. Any final answer to the question is therefore an impossibility, but nevertheless some conclusions of a general character can be reached....

Although the Scriptures do not give any clear word concerning the role of the United States in relationship to the revived Roman Empire and the later development of the world empire, it is probable that the United States will be in some form of alliance with the Roman ruler. Most citizens of the United States of America have come from Europe and their sympathies would be more naturally with a European alliance than with Russia or countries in Eastern Asia. It may even be that the United States will provide large support for the Mediterranean confederacy as it seems to be in opposition to Russia, Eastern Asia, and Africa. Actually a balance of power in the world may exist at that time not too dissimilar to the present world situation, namely, that Europe and the Mediterranean area will be in alliance with America in opposition to Russia, Eastern Asia, and Africa. Based on geographic, religious and economic factors, such an alliance of powers seems a natural sequence of present situations in the world.

If the end-time events include a destruction of Russia and her allies prior to the final period of great tribulation, this may trigger an unbalance in the world situation that will permit the Roman ruler to become a world ruler. In this event, it should be clear that the United States will be in a subordinate role and no longer the great international power that it is today.

It has been suggested by some that the total absence of Scriptural comment on the United States of America in the end time is evidence that the United States previously has been destroyed by an atomic war or some other catastrophic means and therefore no longer is a voice in international affairs. Such a solution, however, overlooks the fact that not only the United States but all of the Americas are omitted from prophecy, and the same is true of Australia. The fact is there are few references to any country at some distance from the Holy Land. The view, therefore, would be preferable that while the United States is in existence and possibly a power to be reckoned with in the rapidly moving events which characterize the end of the age, world political power will be centered in the Mediterranean area and necessarily the United States will play a subordinate role.

History has many records of great nations which have risen to unusual power and influence only to decline because of internal corruption or international complications. It may well be that the United States of America is today at the zenith of its power, much as Babylon was in the sixth century BC prior to its sudden downfall at the hands of the Medes and the Persians (Daniel 5). Any realistic survey of moral conditions in the world today would justify a judgment of God on any nation, including that of the United States. The long-suffering God has offered unusual benefits to the United States both in a material and religious way, but they have been used with such profligacy that ultimate divine judgment may be expected. The question no longer is whether America deserves judgment, but rather why divine judgment has been so long withheld from a nation which has enjoyed so much of God's bounty.

A partial answer may be found in the fact that the United States of America, in spite of its failures, has nevertheless been a source of major Christian testimony in the world and has done more to promote the missionary cause in terms of money and men than any other nation. Although the United States numbers only five percent of the total world population, in the last century probably more than fifty percent of the missionaries and money spent has come from America. In view of the fact that it is God's major purpose in this present age to call out Jew and Gentile to faith in Christ and to have the Gospel preached in all nations, the prosperity which has been true of America has made possible this end and may have been permitted by God to accomplish His holy purposes.

Another important reason for delay in divine judgment upon America is the Abrahamic promise concerning his seed, "I will bless them that bless thee, and curse him that curseth thee" (Genesis 12:3, KJV). The United States, for the most part, has been kind to the Jew. Here the seed of Abraham has had religious freedom and opportunity to make wealth. Judgment on other nations has frequently been preceded by persecution of the Jew. So far in the United States the Jew has had equal treatment.

It is evident, however, that if Christ came for His church and all true Christians were caught out of this world, America then would be reduced to the same situation as other countries. The true church will be gone, and Israel may be persecuted. The drastically changed situation would no longer call for material or political blessing upon the United States. It would therefore follow that with the removal of the principal cause for withholding judgment, namely, the promotion of the missionary cause and befriending the wandering Jew, reason would no longer exist for maintaining America in its present standard of power politically and economically. It may well be that the United

States, like Babylon of old, will lose its place of leadership in the world, and this will be a major cause in the shift of power to the Mediterranean scene.

Although conclusions concerning the role of America in prophecy in the end time are necessarily tentative, the Scriptural evidence is sufficient to conclude that America in that day will not be a major power and apparently does not figure largely in either the political, economic, or religious aspects of the world. America may well be at its zenith today both in power, influence, and opportunity.

From *The Coming Peace in the Middle East*, by Tim LaHaye, 1984

One question recurs with increasing frequency as Russia becomes a more dominant world power: "Is America mentioned in Bible prophecy?" With so many nations of the end time mentioned by name—Egypt, Persia, Iran, Libya, Israel, Russia, and others—it seems reasonable to most students of prophecy that a nation like the United States must be included. Because of America's unique biblical heritage, God's obvious blessing on this country throughout her three-hundred-year history, her worldwide missionary enterprises, and her stature in the world, why wouldn't God include some mention of America during the last days?…

False Thinking About America

The belief that America is not referred to explicitly in the Bible takes some Christians by surprise, for we Americans have a tendency to think of our country as a nation of destiny. The fact is, however, that although we may perceive an allusion or an inference in some prophetic passages, there is no clear-cut reference to America in all the Bible.

On the one hand, we reject the British Israelite theory, but on the other, we presume that God has blessed this country because it was particularly chosen by Him to be His torchbearer in these last two centuries. It seems incredible that a nation so prominent in the last days would not be mentioned somewhere by the prophets.

> Sheba and Dedan and the merchants of Tarshish and all
> her villages will say to you, "Have you come to plunder?
> Have you gathered your hordes to loot, to carry off silver
> and gold, to take away livestock and goods and to seize
> much plunder?" (Ezekiel 38:13)

If an allusion to America appears in Bible prophecy, this is it. If Bible scholars are right and "Tarshish," "Sheba," and "Dedan" represent the Phoenician seafarers who migrated to Great Britain before the time of Christ, America is obliquely referred to here. But I am persuaded that if God really intended to include America in biblical prophecy, He would have been more explicit.

I have read various nationalistic and patriotic statements to the effect that God chose America to be settled by God-fearing people of courage so that He could shower blessings on us which were originally intended for the nation of Israel. As much as I love the United States, I find that theory suspect. First, there is no scriptural evidence for such an idea. Second, it tends to make America the recipient of the covenant promises given to Israel, which is unwarranted biblically. Third, if America does not experience a moral revival soon, her exportation of evil will soon exceed her exportation of the good news of the gospel.

I am not unaware of the testimony of Christopher Columbus and his divine vision regarding the discovery of the Americas. I am familiar with the enormous investments many dedicated American patriots have made in this nation and still are making. Many Christians and other Americans are as fully devoted to the preservation of this nation as any of her founding fathers. If the nation does not regain her moral sanity, it will not be the fault of these patriotic citizens. But we have to look somewhere other than biblical prophecy for the role America plays in the world.

What Is the Secret of America's Greatness?

We need to understand why God has blessed America. It isn't because of her humanitarian treatment of the Indians who preceded us, nor is it for her record on slavery. But she has catalogued a very positive record in several other matters that have incurred the favor of God. Actually the United States has done more things right in the building of the nation than wrong, and God has blessed accordingly.

1. Biblical principles and acknowledgment of God

No matter how zealously present-day secular humanist educators try to distort American history, they cannot alter the fact that America was rooted in more biblical principles than any nation in the history of the world. Why? Because it was founded by more dedicated Christians than any other nation. Atheists do not pioneer the building of a new nation in pursuit of freedom, and enduring the hazards of pioneering is not their style. They prefer to let the Christians build a nation. Then they infiltrate her; alter her laws; take over her government, media, and school system; and change her culture to conform to their human-istic ideas. This has been their program in America, and that is why the nation is currently living on the outskirts of Sodom and Gomorrah.

The Declaration of Independence and most of the other founding documents contain clear recognition of God. The nation's laws are filled with biblical values because the framers of the Constitution were themselves either Christians committed to the Word of God or citizens whose thinking process was saturated with basic Christian values. As Dr. Francis Schaeffer says, they had a "Christian conscience." Most of them came from the part of Europe that had been greatly influenced by the Reformation.

I believe our forefathers clearly intended to incorporate Christian or biblical values in all phases of American life. In so doing, they incurred the blessing of God.

God loves all mankind. He will bless any nation that obeys Him; nationality does not influence His administration of grace. The blessing of God is available to all nations only as a result of obedience. "Blessed rather are those who hear the word of God and obey it" (Luke 11:28).

One reason why I have become so vocal in crying out against the changes imposed on our nation during the last twenty-five years is that most of them conflict with the teaching of the Word of God. If this nation does not halt the secularizing trends of the sixties and seventies, she will soon be as godless as Russia, China, India, Babylon, Persia, and Rome.

2. Religious freedom!

Historically, governments and political leaders have been hostile to religion, particularly religious freedom. Because Americans have enjoyed more religious freedom than any nation in history, we have taken it for granted. In the eighties, however, we have experienced more attacks on religious freedom than any of us thought possible just a few years ago. Who would have believed that the IRS would harass Christian schools? Or that churches could lose their tax deductible status and be forced to pay taxes? Or that government bureaucrats would interfere with the rights of parents to enforce religious values in the raising of their children? Or that a Christian college could be disciplined by the Supreme Court for its interpretation of the Bible regarding interracial marriage? Or ministers could be jailed for running a Christian school in accordance with religious values instead of government values? The list is long.

Our nation's original respect for God, the Bible, and the church incurred the blessing of God for three hundred years of colonial and national history. How else can we explain the victories of the Revolutionary War and the War of 1812? Humanly speaking, our nation snatched victory from the jaws of defeat. We can only account for such events in the light of the blessings of God.

3. Praying, Spirit-filled Christians

Before God decided to destroy Sodom and Gomorrah, He and Abraham engaged in an interesting conversation (Genesis 18:20–33). God agreed to spare the city for forty, twenty, and then ten righteous souls. Unfortunately Sodom and Gomorrah were destroyed because they did not have ten righteous residents. From that account I believe we may draw the premise that God's blessing is extended to a nation in proportion to the percentage of her population that is truly born again. If that be true, America can trace many of her blessings to the fact that she has always had a higher percentage of born-again Christians among her population than any other country. At this stage in American history, it is difficult to say whether that reality will offset the national holocaust created by liberal abortion laws that account for the death of 1.5 million unborn babies each year.

4. America's benevolence and role as peacemaker

Jesus said in Matthew 5:9, "Blessed are the peacemakers, for they will be called sons of God." In 1945 America's military machine conquered Germany and Japan and could easily have gone on to conquer the world. Instead she helped her former enemies rebuild their shattered nations until they were economically her greatest competitors in the world marketplace. In all of history there has never been a more "merciful" nation. God has blessed the United States, not because she is a nation of destiny, but because she has been compassionate.

To a lesser extent, the United States has also been a peacemaking nation until the last few years. Then liberal humanists in power caused her to retreat from her responsibilities and permit Communism to enslave millions. Her failure to give Gen. Douglas MacArthur permission to defend Korea from invasion by Chinese Communists permitted the enslavement of forty million Koreans. Her failure to use military might in Vietnam was a national disgrace, permitting the enslavement or murder of twenty million people. Her vain attempt to enforce the Monroe Doctrine in 1962 permitted Comrade Castro to terrorize many countries in Latin America and even Angola in southwestern Africa. That failure has led to the suffering, murder, and displacement of at least twenty million people.

Before the adoption of this weak foreign policy, the United States enjoyed the blessing of God as a peacemaking nation. Unfortunately the left-wing and humanistic policymakers in the State Department seem to believe that national weakness for us in the face of Communist Russia's inhumane program of world conquest is a virtue. But that flies in the face of both history and common sense. In Luke 11:21–22 Jesus taught the opposite.

> When a strong man, fully armed, guards his own house,
> his possessions are safe. But when someone stronger

attacks and overpowers him, he takes away the armor in
which the man trusted and divides up the spoils.

This sounds like the familiar motto "peace through strength."

5. Her national policy toward Israel

Of all the reasons why God has blessed America, none is more significant than her three-hundred-year history of benevolence toward the
Jews. God promised Abraham, "I will bless those who bless you, and
whoever curses you I will curse; and all peoples on earth will be blessed
through you" (Genesis 12:3). No other nation in history has exceeded
her record of charity extended to the sons of Abraham, Isaac, and
Jacob. I consider this America's best line of national defense.

Let me explain this. Some people complain that Israel receives too
much from the United States' defense budget—more than $4 billion
in 1983. These people suggest that we would better serve our nation
by giving that money to the poor or to a larger nation. But I believe
that the stronger we make Israel, the safer we are as a nation.

One reason is that no one knows how powerful the Soviet Union
really is. Even our intelligence-gathering services—hampered as they
are by congressional restraints—are unreliable, as the Grenadan invasion of 1983 disclosed. It would be possible for a U.S. president to be
blackmailed into submitting to a Communist takeover out of fear of
Russian supremacy. The Communists are consummate bluffers and
masters of "misinformation." The tragedy of the twentieth century
could well be the unnecessary capitulation to Communist slavery by
naive leaders in the United States in the face of what they thought was
nuclear superiority and first-strike destruction, but in reality was a
paper tiger.

As long as there is a strong Israeli air force with the capability of nuclear retaliation, Russia will not attack the United States. Israel is the Achilles' heel to the Soviets' designs for world supremacy. Before they can suppress the world with their totalitarian ideology, they must first knock out the United States. And to do that, they must first remove Israel.

Thus Israel's safety and military strength are our own nation's best interest for survival. Why should we not supply them with F-15s and F-16s, our latest weapons systems, air-to-air refueling capabilities, and even missiles, ICBMs, or anything else that makes Israel a threat to Russia? It is not that Russia (the No. 1 superpower) has need to fear Israel (the third most powerful military force) herself; rather, she must fear Nos. 2 and 3 simultaneously.

Another reason is that, although we spend less in the defense of Israel than we do in Europe and Japan, we get a greater return on our investment. Europe has as many people as the United States, but she seems to have little stamina for standing up to the Soviet Union. Her leaders criticize us when we oppose the Communists. When U.S. marines invaded Grenada, for example, we received nothing but abuse from our European allies.

And what about our Japanese allies, whom the United States has been protecting from Chinese and Russia communism for four decades? Because of American aid, Japan has been able to divert its resources and technology from the national defense to consumer goods—automobiles, radios, and computers—often to the detriment of our own economy.

Of all our allies, Israel is the only one we can depend on in a time of crisis. Why? (1) Because our survival is vital to her own; (2) because there are three times as many Jews in the United States as there are in Israel; and (3) because she is the only other nation besides ours that has the potential for military retaliation against a Russian attack.

We get more results from the dollars we spend in building a strong defense for Israel than we do from any others. Israel has already demonstrated its will to fight when attacked. We don't have to agree with everything Israel does to realize that defending her is a good investment in our own best interests.

I further believe that we as a people have enjoyed more years of free elections—more than two hundred years of them—than any other nation. We have experienced more religious freedom and more prosperity, because we have recognized that the Jews are God's chosen people and the special objects of His love—not because they deserve it, but because He chose them even before the first Jew, Jacob, was born. Jews were welcomed in America during her colonial days and have enjoyed more freedom here than they have ever been granted before. That no doubt explains why at least 55 percent of the world's Jews reside in America. There are almost as many Jews in New York City (3 million) as in Israel (3.5 million).

In the United States, Jews share the rights and privileges of all her citizens. They can freely own land, run for public office, enjoy unparalleled religious freedom, manage banks and businesses, and live a discrimination-free life. The little persecution of Jews that occurs is always met with community outrage, and the courts and law enforcement officers restrain such individuals. Anti-Semitism is not condoned in this country, and one hopes it never will be.

Christians—Israel's Best Friend

It is no accident that the country with the world's best treatment of the Jews was founded on more Christian principles than any other nation and has more Christians (69 million: Gallup Poll) than any other. Born-again Christians who know their Bible have always been

Israel's best friend. Admittedly, some in history who were identified as Christians have persecuted the Jews, but they were not biblically taught. True believers recognize God's covenant with Israel and use their influence to perpetuate the national humanitarian treatment of them as a people, thus incurring the blessing of God.

America to the rescue, 1940–1945

I was never more proud of my country than when I stood at the museum in a German concentration camp in Dachau, Germany, studying the photographs of the atrocities inflicted there under the Nazi regime. Adolf Hitler began imprisoning the Jews in 1936. Pictures taken on the way to captivity show them plump, well-dressed, and not seriously concerned. The pictures of 1938 testify that the imprisonments intensified and the starvation and persecution of the inmates increased. By 1945 the Jews were literally skeletons with skin but without flesh. However, the haunting looks on those emaciated faces suddenly turned to excited joy. What had happened? American GIs had come to rescue them.

The United States has not only provided a welcome haven for the Jews in our homeland, but has rescued three-fourths of the world's Jews from certain annihilation. That mad dictator, Hitler, intended to wipe out all the Jews in Europe and Russia. At that time, three-fourths of the world's Jews lived within the borders of the countries Hitler would have conquered—if America had not entered the war.

There is no question in my mind that we have enjoyed unprecedented blessing from God in this country because of our treatment of the Jews. How long that character will offset the humanist-inspired practices of abortion on demand, homosexual acceptance, pornography, and continual secularization of our society I do not know. But in my heart I am convinced that if we ever change our policy toward the Jews, we will become like Sodom and Gomorrah.

Israel right or wrong?

The national policy of the United States toward Israel does not support everything that nation does. We Christians must remember that many of Israel's leaders are Zionists; consequently some of them are as secular as America's humanists. If some Zionists had their way, they would close the synagogues and do away with many time-honored Jewish customs. In addition, Zionist-inspired dealings with the Arab residents of Israel do not always show respect for human rights. If they were to become inhumane in their treatment of the Arabs, the United States would have to reevaluate her policies toward Israel. I hope that we as a people will never be found guilty of mistreating the Jews as individuals.

As a nation, Israel inhabits the land largely in unbelief. Not until Russia is supernaturally destroyed by God on the mountains of Israel will the nation turn en masse to Him. Until then, we must treat Israel as a trusted ally and judge her on the merits of her conduct—but always treating individual Jews with compassion.

What All This Means

We learn from all these experiences that America has historically enjoyed the blessings of God, not because she was a nation of destiny or is mentioned in biblical prophecy, but because our founding fathers were so biblically oriented in their thinking that they established a country whose conduct pleased God. Any other country following these policies will enjoy the same blessings. A good example is Canada. She is second only to the United States in her record of following biblical principles and of favorable treatment of Jews; thus she too has enjoyed the blessings of God.

England, on the other hand, has fallen on hard times after centuries of national blessing. Many prophecy students feel that England turned her back on Israel during the thirties and particularly in 1945 and 1946, when she withdrew entirely from Palestine. Consequently she is reaping the results today. In addition, consider England's record on religious freedom and commitment. Four percent of the English people go to church. The government will not permit the construction of a Christian radio or television station there (whereas the United States has more than one thousand Christian radio stations and more than fifty Christian TV stations). Secular humanists exercise more control over national affairs in England than they do in America. That's why their government policy is more secular.

Three confederations of nations

Scripture identifies three confederations of nations in the last days. The two that we have already examined will be involved in the invasion of Israel: the northeastern confederation, consisting of "Russia and her hordes," and the western democracies that send the diplomatic note of Ezekiel 38:13. In all probability Israel is part of the latter confederation, forsaken by her allies just before God intervenes.

Possibly, however, a third confederation may exist at the time of the invasion—or at least a group that will have the capability of being a confederation. "The kings of the East," the nations east of the Euphrates, will march on Israel at the close of the tribulation period, when all the world will attack Christ in "the battle on the great day of God Almighty," known more popularly as the Battle of Armageddon (Revelation 16:12–14). These nations will include China, India, Japan, and other oriental countries. What do they have in common? Eastern religious philosophy—which expresses itself in society in ways similar to secular humanism—and hatred for Christianity and the Bible.

Because the Bible includes these three confederations as players on the world stage in the last days, we can assume that America is included.

At present the worldwide presence of the United States assures that Russia will not rule the world at the end time prior to her attempt to take Israel. The only human instrument that currently keeps Russia from conquering the world is the strength of the United States. This would indicate that America will coexist with Russia right up to the end, but will probably not have any more supremacy over her than we do today. That is, America would be one of the western democracies that sends the diplomatic note to Russia just before the attempted invasion of Israel.

The Future of America

It is not difficult to predict the future of America. Unless we experience a moral revival and shake off the domination of the secular humanists who control our government, media, and public education, we will be a fifth-rate power in twenty to thirty years. Does that sound like an extreme statement? I suggest you draw a simple graph of our national decline during the past thirty years and project the same rate of decline for the next thirty. We can apply that graph to the nation's morals, military might, economy, religious freedom, and family breakdown. On the increase are the size of government, taxation, secular humanist propaganda, crime, drugs, VD, pornography, Communist subversion, and a host of other harmful social influences. America will no longer be the America most of us inherited thirty years ago if we continue to decline at the present rate....

Is There Hope for America?

Yes, there is hope for America. As long as life persists, under God we can hope. But that hope will never come to fruition if we continue to violate the moral laws of God.

The only hope for America is a moral revival—a national recognition of her sins against God and her fellowmen and a return to the traditional moral values upon which the nation was founded. I believe that such a revival could happen very soon. Several of the nation's religious leaders have personally expressed to me, in public or in private, a belief that revival is coming.

Something unusual has occurred during the past thirty years in the United States. While she has experienced the moral decline already described, she has also reaped the largest soul harvest and church growth in her history. Surveys suggest that there are almost three times as many born-again Christians in the nation today as there were thirty years ago. The conditions producing this amazing growth may generate three times the soul harvest during the next three decades. If the Gallup Poll is right and the nation indeed has 69 million born-again citizens, that number could jump to 130 million by the year 2000. If that happens, the majority of our population may be Christian by then.

Admittedly, numbers are speculative. But if enough of the morally committed citizens of the United States will involve themselves in the electoral process by either running for public offices or helping those who share our traditional values get elected, we can rid our government of the secular humanists who are destroying the nation. Such a change in government leadership is possible in one decade, and that is essential to revival, for the humanists in the political and judicial systems have consistently legislated for sin and against civil morality. Currently they seek to stifle religious freedom. The renowned constitutional attorney, William Ball, has stated, "We no longer have religious freedom in this country; we have religious toleration." If Christians do not take a more active part in the electoral process, both as candidates and as campaign workers, these humanists will transform religious toleration into religious intolerance.…

Will Russia Destroy America?

I am frequently asked, "Will Russia conquer the United States before she attempts to invade Israel?" The Bible does not provide an answer, but I have an opinion: "I seriously doubt it." I have stated my reasons already in this book. In short, if America were conquered, nothing could stop Russia from subjugating the whole world. But the prophets make it clear that Russia will attack Israel before a one-world government is formed. I believe that Russia and America will continue to function at parity until Russia becomes powerful enough to defy the U.S. and attack Israel. This will create a vacuum into which the secular humanist advocates of the new world order will move quickly, forming the one-world government of the end time.

Our national policy of humane treatment of the Jews, if unchanged, will keep America from being conquered by Russia. Historically speaking, a nation that was evil to the Jews has never conquered a nation that was good to Israel. The United States' best line of national defense remains her favorable treatment of individual Jews and her national defense of her ally Israel.

Will America Be Destroyed by a Nuclear Bomb?

Again, it is impossible to be dogmatic, because the Bible is silent on this subject. However, Christ will return to a well-populated world. I am inclined to believe that the present stalemate of nuclear weapons will continue until the Lord comes. And in that case Christ will come soon. It is frighteningly conceivable that some mad terrorist or Idi Amin–type of dictator could gain control of a nuclear bomb and threaten to destroy the world. The only sure preventative is the second coming of Christ.

The most important words to contemplate on this subject come from our Lord Himself:

> Therefore keep watch, because you do not know on what
> day your Lord will come. But understand this: If the owner
> of the house had known at what time of night the thief was
> coming, he would have kept watch and would not have let
> his house be broken into. (Matthew 24:42–43)

FREQUENTLY ASKED QUESTIONS

1. After spiritual preparation, what's the most important thing Americans can do to prepare for the future?

While there are many legitimate answers to this question, I would suggest simplifying your life. One of the chief causes of our nation's troubles is excess. When crises come, most people are woefully ill prepared because they are stretched too far financially. Most Americans need to commit to saving more and spending less. To living within their means. To traveling lighter through life. This kind of life brings less stress, greater freedom and flexibility, and the opportunity to be in a better position to weather personal storms as well as have some disposable funds to help others in need. Simplifying our lives will mean different things to different people, the people I know who live simple, uncluttered lives are always in the best position to face the future, whatever it brings.

2. How can we become better at combining biblical knowledge with cultural awareness?

In 1 Chronicles 12:32 we read about a rare, valuable breed of men in the days of King David: "the sons of Issachar, men who understood the times, with knowledge of what Israel should do." These men discerned the times and cast their lot with David instead of Saul, which proved to be a very wise decision. We should strive to be modern "sons of Issachar" who understand our times and are able to parlay that knowledge into practical action for our lives, our families, our communities, and our nation. I don't think this means that we have to be twenty-four-hour news junkies who eagerly gobble up every cable news story or constantly comb the Internet for breaking news. It simply means that we cannot be social or civic ostriches with heads buried in the Bible, unaware of the issues and challenges of our day.

But how can we become modern-day Issacharites? How can we bring God's wisdom to bear in our increasingly polarized political environment? Let me suggest a couple of things. First, understanding of the times means we should be familiarizing ourselves with both sides of the issues and the real challenges of our day. To do this I would suggest thoughtfully reading a daily newspaper, listening to one good news program regularly that involves analysis and presents views opposite your own, and becoming intentional about reading good books that heighten and inform your cultural awareness. Second, it also means that we must not be afraid to actively, creatively, discerningly engage and embrace our culture as led by the Holy Spirit.

3. How do you suggest people overcome any fears they have of the future?

The first decade of the twenty-first century is over, and many people are grateful. Experts have given the decade a resounding thumbs-down. It's been dubbed by many as the decade of fear or even the lost decade. It started with the horror of 9/11 and the ongoing war on terror, was punctuated by two serious recessions, raised the specter of climate crisis, and ended with unemployment hovering around 10 percent. How can we be optimistic about the future?

While no one on earth knows what the future holds, we can know who holds the future. That's our solace in uncertain, dangerous times. My favorite word in all of Bible prophecy is a name for God. I call it the prophetic name for God. God is called "the Almighty" nine times in the book of Revelation. The English word comes from the Greek *pantokrator,* which is made up of *pantos* (all) and *kratein* (to hold in one's hand). God has everything in His hands. Next time you are tempted by fear or a nagging pessimism about the future, let this thought flood your soul: God holds everything. No matter how things appear, He really does. That includes our nation, our families, and our lives.

NOTES

Chapter 1

1. Nancy Gibbs, "Apocalypse Now," *Time,* July 1, 2002, 42–48.

2. Thomas Ice and Timothy Demy, *The Truth About America in the Last Days* (Eugene, OR: Harvest House, 1998), 7.

3. Frances Rolleston, *Notes on the Apocalypse, as Explained by the Hebrew Scriptures: The Place in Prophecy of America and Australia Being Pointed Out* (London: Rivingtons, 1858).

4. Uriah Smith, *The United States in the Light of Prophecy; or, An Exposition of Rev. 13:11–17* (Battle Creek, MI: Seventh-Day Adventist Publishing, 1884), v.

5. Peggy Noonan, "A Separate Peace: America is in trouble—and our elites are merely resigned," *Wall Street Journal,* September 27, 2005, www.opinion journal.com/columnists/pnoonan/?id=110007460.

Chapter 2

1. S. Franklin Logsdon, *Is the U.S.A. in Prophecy?* (Grand Rapids, MI: Zondervan, 1968), 9. This same view is presented in Edward Tracy, *The United States in Prophecy* (Pine Grove, CA: Convale, 1969).

2. Logsdon, *Is the U.S.A. in Prophecy?* 59–60. Note that Logsdon's work was published in 1968 during the height of the cold war between the U.S. and the Soviet Union. Edward Tracy's book, *The United States in Prophecy,* supports Logsdon's thesis that the United States is the Babylon of the end times.

3. Jack Van Impe, *The Great Escape* (Nashville: Word, 1998), 207.

4. Jack Van Impe, *2001: On the Edge of Eternity* (Dallas: Word, 1996), 179.

5. Adapted from R. A. Coombes, *America, the Babylon* (Liberty, MO: Real Publishing, 1998), 55–58.

6. Adapted from Coombes, *America, the Babylon,* 182–86.

7. Charles H. Dyer, *The Rise of Babylon: Sign of the End Times* (Wheaton, IL: Tyndale, 1991), 182.

8. Robert L. Thomas, *Revelation 8–22: An Exegetical Commentary* (Chicago: Moody, 1995), 307.

9. Charles H. Dyer, "The Identity of Babylon in Revelation 17–18," *Bibliotheca Sacra* 144 (October–December 1987): 441–43.

10. For more information about this view, see Mark Hitchcock, *The Second Coming of Babylon: What Bible Prophecy Says About…* (Sisters, OR: Multnomah, 2003).

11. Joseph A. Seiss, *The Last Times and the Great Consummation: An Earnest Discussion of Momentous Themes,* rev. ed. (Philadelphia: Smith, English & Co., 1863), 200. This work was originally published in 1856. Cf. Paul Richard Wilkinson, *For Zion's Sake: Christian Zionism and the Role of John Nelson Darby,* Studies in Evangelical History and Thought (Colorado Springs: Paternoster, 2007), 239.

12. Seiss, *Last Times and the Great Consummation,* 200.

13. Van Impe, *Great Escape,* 206.

14. E. F. Webber, *America in Prophecy* (Oklahoma City: Southwest Radio Church, 1993), 6. Webber lists eight points from Isaiah 18:1–2 that he believes identify the United States with this unnamed nation (3–6).

15. Herbert W. Armstrong, *The United States and Britain in Prophecy* (USA: Worldwide Church of God, 1986), 96.

16. Armstrong, *United States and Britain in Prophecy,* 96.

17. Armstrong, *United States and Britain in Prophecy,* 98.

18. Armstrong, *United States and Britain in Prophecy,* 104.

19. Edwin Yamauchi, "Ezra, Nehemiah," in *The Expositor's Bible Commentary*, ed. Frank E. Gaebelein, vol. 4 (Grand Rapids, MI: Zondervan, 1988), 606.

20. Jeffrey Louie, "An Expositional Study of the 144,000 in the Book of the Revelation" (PhD diss., Dallas Theological Seminary, 1990), 38.

21. Louie, "Expositional Study of the 144,000," 39–40.

22. Louie, "Expositional Study of the 144,000," 41.

23. Some maintain that the 144,000 witnesses in Revelation 7:1–8 are the same as the innumerable multitude in Revelation 7:9–17. See Hank Hanegraaff, *The Apocalypse Code* (Nashville: Thomas Nelson, 2007), 125. However, nothing in the context supports the idea that the 144,000 and the great multitude are one and the same. (1) The 144,000 were carefully numbered as twelve groups of 12,000, while the second group is innumerable, "which no one could count." How could it be that a precise number is given to the group of Jewish men, while the second group is said to be so vast that it would be impossible for people to count them, if they are supposed to be the same group? (2) The first group was said to be Jews "from every tribe of the sons of Israel," while the second group is said to be from "every nation and all tribes and peoples and tongues." (3) The 144,000 are sealed in order to protect them from the impending trumpet judgments about to befall planet earth, while the great multitude has been delivered from the impending wrath through martyrdom and are safely in heaven.

If these are two different groups, then an interesting and exciting relationship is implied between them. Israel's calling was to be a light to the nations. It has thus far not done a very good job of fulfilling that calling. However, in the Tribulation, Israel will make progress toward becoming that light to the Gentiles that it was set apart to become. The 144,000 Jewish men will be like thousands of apostle Pauls, out evangelizing the nations. The result will be millions of conversions to

Christ among the Gentiles, even though many will have to give their lives, contributing to the great multitude described in verse 9. The 144,000 Jews, like Paul, are supernaturally converted at some point after the Rapture of the church. Since the Rapture will leave believers without mature leadership—all true believers will be taken in the Rapture—the supernatural protection of God's seal will enable the 144,000 to become fearless preachers of the gospel during such a physically demanding time. This cause-effect view better explains Revelation 7 than Hanegraaff's both-and view.

24. Norman L. Geisler, "Review of Hank Hanegraaff's *The Apocalypse Code*," Southern Evangelical Seminary www.ses.edu/NormanGeisler/ReviewApocalypseCode.html.

25. Notice that Iraq and Egypt are missing from this list. This is significant in light of Egypt's peace with Israel forged in 1979 and the U.S. involvement in Iraq. The omission of Egypt and Iraq from this invading coalition fits what we see today.

26. Arnold G. Fruchtenbaum, *The Footsteps of the Messiah: A Study of the Sequence of Prophetic Events,* rev. ed. (Tustin, CA: Ariel Ministries, 2003), 111–12.

27. Fruchtenbaum, *Footsteps of the Messiah,* 111.

28. Fruchtenbaum, *Footsteps of the Messiah,* 112.

29. Ed Hindson, *Is the Antichrist Alive and Well?* (Eugene, OR: Harvest House, 1998), 127.

30. Van Impe, *2001,* 178.

31. David Allen Lewis, *Prophecy 2000* (Green Forest, AR: New Leaf, 1990), 101, 103.

Chapter 3

1. Herman Hoyt, *Is the United States in Prophecy?* (Winona Lake, IN: BMH Books, 1977), 2.

2. Tim LaHaye, "Is the United States in Bible Prophecy?" *National Liberty Journal,* 26 (February 1997): 16.

3. Hoyt, *Is the United States in Prophecy?* 6.

4. John F. Walvoord, *The Nations in Prophecy* (Grand Rapids, MI: Zondervan, 1967), 175.

5. Charles C. Ryrie, *The Best Is Yet to Come* (Chicago: Moody, 1981), 109–10.

Chapter 4

1. You can find additional information about the place oil may play in the end times in a book I coauthored, *Armageddon, Oil and Terror* (Wheaton, IL: Tyndale, 2007).

2. Peter Tertzakian, *A Thousand Barrels a Second: The Coming Oil Break Point and the Challenges Facing an Energy Dependent World* (New York: McGraw-Hill, 2006), 3.

3. Scott Burns, "How much oil it'd take to buy the U.S.," MSN Money, July 16, 2008, http://articles.moneycentral.msn.com/Investing/Extra/ HowMuchOilItd TakeToBuyTheUS.aspx.

4. Most figures from Robert Samuelson, "The Triumph of OPEC," *Newsweek,* March 17, 2008, 45.

5. Samuelson, "Triumph of OPEC," 45.

6. Fareed Zakaria, "A Marine's New Mission," *Newsweek,* February 11, 2008, www.newsweek.com/id/107577.

7. Zakaria, "A Marine's New Mission."

8. Zakaria, "A Marine's New Mission."

9. Zakaria, "A Marine's New Mission."

10. David Lynch, "Debate Brews: Has Oil Production Peaked?" *USA Today,* October 16, 2005, http://peakoil.blogspot.com/2005/10/debate-brews -has-oil-production-peaked.html.

11. Neil King Jr. and Spencer Swartz, "Oil Exporters Are Unable to Keep Up with Demand," *Wall Street Journal,* May 29, 2008.

12. Lester R. Brown, "Is World Oil Production Peaking?" Earth Policy Institute, November 15, 2007, www.earth-policy.org/Updates/2007/Update67.htm. Some experts, such as Daniel Yergin and Peter Jackson, contend that there's plenty more oil out there and that the peak of production won't occur until at least 2020. They also point out that even when the peak is reached, there won't be an immediate plummet but several years of coasting on a kind of "undulating plateau." David Lynch, "Debate Brews: Has Oil Production Peaked?" *USA Today,* October 16, 2005. While the debate continues about the timing of the peak, there seems to be general agreement that oil is a finite resource and that the world is consuming more oil than it discovers. And while it is true that much more oil may be discovered, it may be so expensive to retrieve it that its not economically feasible to get it out of the ground.

13. Brown, "Is World Oil Production Peaking?"

14. Linda Stern, "Don't Get Pumped Dry," *Newsweek,* April 14, 2008, 81.

15. Brown, "Is World Oil Production Peaking?"

16. Lynch, "Debate Brews."

17. "Peak Oil: Life After the Crash," www.lifeaftertheoilcrash.net/.

18. "Black Gold: Coal price spikes top oil," *Daily Oklahoman,* April 1, 2008.

19. Fareed Zakaria, "Why We Can't Quit," *Newsweek,* March 24, 2008, 40, www.newsweek.com/id/123482.

20. Lynch, "Debate Brews."

21. Zakaria, "Why We Can't Quit," 40.

22. Zakaria, "Why We Can't Quit," 40.

23. Stevenson Jacobs, "Why groceries could cost more soon," *Daily Oklahoman,* April 4, 2008.

24. Michael Grunwald, "The Clean Energy Myth," *Time,* April 7, 2008, 40–45. The information in the section on biofuels was taken from this article.

25. Grunwald, "Clean Energy Myth," 44.

26. Jacobs, "Why groceries could cost more soon."

27. Jacobs, "Why groceries could cost more soon."

28. Grunwald, "Clean Energy Myth."

29. Russell Blinch and Brian Love, "Tensions rise as world faces short rations," Reuters, March 31, 2008.

30. Andrew Leonard, "North Dakota—not quite ready for OPEC prime time," Salon.com, April 10, 2008.

31. Jack Money, "What's the Alternative? Pickens says wind power may be the future," *Daily Oklahoman,* April 24, 2008.

32. Money, "What's the Alternative?"

33. Michael Klare, "Oil and the 'New International Energy Order,'" NPR, April 14, 2008, www.npr.org/templates/story/story.php?storyId =89565453.

34. Tertzakian, *A Thousand Barrels a Second,* xii–xiii.

35. Fox News, "Ahmadinejad calls U.S. 'satanic,' Israel 'about to die,'" June 2, 2008, www.foxnews.com/story/0,2933,361705,00.html.

Chapter 5

1. Dunstan Prial, "Sovereign Wealth Funds Leveraged Against U.S. Regulators," Fox Business, February 29, 2008.

2. Peter Navarro, "Sovereign Wealth Funds: China's Potent Economic Weapon," *Christian Science Monitor,* February 8, 2008, www.csmonitor .com/ 2008/0208/p09s01-coop.html.

3. The Becker-Posner Blog, December 10, 2007, www.becker-posner-blog .com/archives/2007/12/sovereignwealth.html.

4. Michael Schuman, "America's Coming Garage Sale," *Time,* March 24, 2008, www.time.com/time/magazine/article/0,9171,1725094,00.html.

5. Schuman, "America's Coming Garage Sale."

6. Navarro, "Sovereign Wealth Funds."

7. Fareed Zakaria, "A Marine's New Mission," *Newsweek,* February 11, 2008, www.newsweek.com/id/107577.

8. Adam Davidson, "U.S. Watches Nervously as Oil-Rich Nations Invest," NPR, November 30, 2007, www.npr.org/templates/story/story.php ?storyId=16759653.

9. Davidson, "U.S. Watches Nervously."

10. Davidson, "U.S. Watches Nervously."

11. Tim LaHaye, "The Three Unmistakable Signs of the End Times," *Pre-Trib Perspectives* (February 2008): 3.

12. Robert J. Samuelson, "The Great Shopping Spree, R.I.P.," *Newsweek,* April 28, 2008, 49.

13. Justin Fox, "The New Austerity," *Time,* March 24, 2008, 56.

14. Associated Press, "Air Force: U.S. Domination of Skies at Risk," February 18, 2008, www.msnbc.msn.com/id/23223286/.

15. As related and quoted by Schuman, "America's Coming Garage Sale."

16. Peter G. Peterson, "You Can't Take It with You," *Newsweek,* April 7, 2008, 56.

17. Richard Wolf, "Officials Warn of Medicare's Demise," *USA Today,* March 26, 2008.

18. George Tenet, *At the Center of the Storm: My Years at the CIA* (New York: HarperCollins, 2007), 270.

Chapter 6

1. Lev Grossman, "Apocalypse New," *Time,* January 28, 2008, 211.

2. Nina Hachigian and Mona Sutphen, *The Next American Century* (New York: Simon & Schuster, 2008), 47.

3. Hachigian and Sutphen, *Next American Century,* 48.

4. Hachigian and Sutphen, *Next American Century,* 48–49.

5. Hachigian and Sutphen, *Next American Century,* 49.

6. Hachigian and Sutphen, *Next American Century,* 48. Jerome Corsi

presents evidence of China's military buildup and argues that China's strong economic growth will make it possible to build one of the most modern armies in the world. See Corsi, *The Late Great U.S.A.* (Los Angeles: World Ahead Media, 2007), 162–65.

7. Hachigian and Sutphen, *Next American Century,* 48.

8. George Tenet, *At the Center of the Storm: My Years at the CIA* (New York: HarperCollins, 2007), 259.

9. Tenet, *Center of the Storm,* 259–60.

10. Tenet, *Center of the Storm,* 269.

11. Tenet, *Center of the Storm,* 269.

12. Tenet, *Center of the Storm,* 268.

13. Hachigian and Sutphen, *Next American Century,* 33.

14. Tenet, *Center of the Storm,* 261.

15. The Lugar Letter, July 2005, www.lugar.senate.gov/newsletter/.

16. "Experts Warn of Future WMD Attack," CBS News, June 22, 2005, www.cbsnews.com.

17. Graham Allison, "How Likely Is a Nuclear Terrorist Attack on the United States?" Council on Foreign Relations, February 28, 2008, www.cfr.org/publication/13097.

18. Allison, "How Likely Is a Nuclear Terrorist Attack?"

19. Karen DeYoung, "Tenet Details Efforts to Justify Invading Iraq," *Washington Post,* April 27, 2007.

20. Hachigian and Sutphen, *Next American Century,* 34.

21. Allison, "How Likely Is a Nuclear Terrorist Attack?"

22. Allison, "How Likely Is a Nuclear Terrorist Attack?"

23. Allison, "How Likely Is a Nuclear Terrorist Attack?"

24. Allison, "How Likely Is a Nuclear Terrorist Attack?"

25. "Study Details Catastrophic Impact of Nuclear Attack on U.S. Cities" *Science Daily,* March 21, 2007, www.sciencedaily.com/releases/2007/03/070320103821.htm.

26. "Study Details Catastrophic Impact."

27. Allison, "How Likely Is a Nuclear Terrorist Attack?"

28. Lisa Beyer, "Roots of Rage," *Time,* October 1, 2001, 45.

29. Kevin Peraino, "The Fox Is Hunted Down," *Newsweek,* February 25, 2008, 42.

30. Editorial, *Dallas Morning News,* November 27, 1991.

Chapter 7

1. James Montgomery Boice, *Romans,* 4 vols. (Grand Rapids, MI: Baker, 1991), 1:179.

2. *World,* March 22/29, 2008, 18. This statistic comes from a report from the Centers for Disease Control and Prevention.

3. Zenit News Agency, "The latest marriage statistics: implications," AD2000, October 2005, www.ad2000.com.au/articles/2005/oct2005p8_2076.html.

4. First Things First, "Out-of-Wedlock Pregnancy Fact Sheet," http://first things first.org/page/research/out-of-wedlock-pregnancy-fact-sheet.

5. Emily Yoffe, "…And Baby Makes Two," Slate, March 20, 2008, www.slate.com/id/2185944/.

6. Herman Hoyt, *Is the United States in Prophecy?* (Winona Lake, IN: BMH Books, 1977), 2.

7. John Walvoord, *The Nations in Prophecy* (Grand Rapids, MI: Zondervan, 1967), 174.

8. William Hendriksen, *Romans,* New Testament Commentary (Grand Rapids, MI: Baker, 1980), 75.

9. Frederic Godet, *Commentary on St. Paul's Epistle to the Romans,* vol. 1 (Reprint, Grand Rapids, MI: Kregel, 1977), 177.

10. Douglas J. Moo, *The Epistle to the Romans,* New International Commentary on the New Testament (Grand Rapids, MI: Eerdmans, 1996), 111.

11. R. C. Sproul, *Romans,* Focus on the Bible (Scotland: Christian Focus Publications, 1994), 45.

12. Some of the better-known teachers who hold this view are Ray Stedman, *From Guilt to Glory,* (Palo Alto, CA: Discovery, 1978), 1:38–46; Sproul, *Romans,* 45–50; Chuck Smith, *The Gospel According to Grace* (Costa Mesa, CA: Word for Today, 1981), 11–14; and John R. W. Stott, *Romans: God's Good News for the World* (Downers Grove, IL: InterVarsity, 1994), 76.

13. Stedman, *From Guilt to Glory,* 1:39.

14. Joshua Alston, "Sex on TV: Was It Good for You?" *Newsweek,* June 9, 2008, 59.

15. Alston, "Sex on TV."

16. Some dispute that Paul here is dealing with homosexuality. For an excellent defense of the traditional view, see Stott, *Romans,* 76–78.

17. Stedman, *From Guilt to Glory,* 1:42.

18. Charles Hodge, *Commentary on the Epistle to the Romans* (1837 Reprint, Grand Rapids, MI: Eerdmans, 1983), 42.

19. Kathy Belge, "Prevalence of Bisexuality and Lesbianism in the U.S.," http://lesbianlife.about.com/od/lesbiansex/a/SameSexBehavior.htm.

20. Anna Quindlen, "The Same People," *Newsweek,* June 9, 2008, 70, www.newsweek.com/id/139423/page/1.

21. Sproul, *Romans,* 46–47.

22. Sproul, *Romans,* 46.

23. Donald Grey Barnhouse, *Romans,* (Grand Rapids, MI: Eerdmans, 1952), 1:276–77.

24. Sproul, *Romans,* 47.

25. Hendriksen, *Romans,* 78.

26. Boice, *Romans,* 1:183.

27. S. Lewis Johnson, "Romans," SLJ Institute, www.sljinstitute.net.

Chapter 8

1. For a thorough discussion of the Rapture and the various views about its timing, see Mark Hitchcock, *Could the Rapture Happen Today?* (Sisters, OR: Multnomah Books, 2005).

2. The Barna Group, "Born Again Christians," www.barna.org/FlexPage .aspx?Page= Topic&TopicID=8.

3. The Barna Group "Is American Christianity Turning Charismatic," January 7, 2008, www.barna.org/FlexPage.aspx?Page=BarnaUpdate NarrowPreview&Barna UpdateID=287.

4. There are certainly many nonevangelicals and Catholics who are true believers in Christ, and there are certainly some who claim to be evangelicals who are not true believers. However, I have chosen to use these statistics because they provide at least a general picture of the spiritual landscape in various nations and the effect that the Rapture will have when it occurs. See Patrick Johnstone, *Operation World*, 4th ed. (Grand Rapids, MI: Zondervan, 1987).

5. This raises the issue of what happens to children and babies when the Rapture occurs. As one could imagine, this question is frequently asked by parents with small children. Believing parents want to know if their young children who have not yet trusted Christ will be left behind at the Rapture. It is important at the outset to note that there is no specific Scripture that addresses this subject. Nevertheless, there are three main views on this issue.

   View #1: No children will be included in the Rapture. Those who hold this view would emphasize that the Rapture is only for believers and that if a person has not personally believed in Christ he or she is not eligible for the Rapture. They would point out that in the flood and destruction of the inhabitants of Canaan, small children were not excluded from the judgment.

   View #2: All infants and young children will be raptured to heaven before the Tribulation. Those who hold this view would be quick to point out that Scripture strongly implies that when young children die they go to heaven. Several passages in the Bible seem to support this position: 2 Samuel 12:20–23; Matthew 19:13–15; Mark 10:13–16. Since all young children or infants who have never put saving faith in Christ go to heaven when they die, many would argue that they will also go to heaven in the Rapture and be exempted from the horrors of the Tribulation. This is the view presented in the Left Behind series. All children under the age of twelve are raptured regardless of the spiritual condition of their parents. While I agree that infants and small children who die go to heaven to be with Christ, I do not believe that this necessarily means that they will participate in the Rapture. These are two different issues.

View #3: Infants and young children of believers will be raptured to heaven before the Tribulation. This is a mediating view between Views 1 and 2. While one should avoid dogmatism on this issue, I believe this is the best view for two reasons. First, 1 Corinthians 7:14 reminds us that, in a Christian family, the children are set apart for the Lord. It seems inconceivable to me that the Lord would Rapture believing parents to heaven and leave their defenseless children alone in the world for the Tribulation period. Second, I believe there is biblical precedent for this view. When the Lord sent the flood on the earth during the days of Noah, all the world was destroyed, including unbelieving men, women, and children. But God delivered Noah, his wife, and his three sons and their wives. Likewise when God destroyed Sodom and Gomorrah, He destroyed all the inhabitants of the cities, including the children of unbelievers. The only ones to escape were Lot and his two daughters. Also, in Egypt at the first Passover, the homes of believers, including their young children, were protected from the judgment of God by the blood of the lamb on the doorpost. In each of these cases, the believer and his children were delivered from the time of judgment while unbelievers and their children were not. While I recognize that Noah's three sons and Lot's daughters were not infants or small children and were probably believers themselves, I believe that these incidents provide biblical precedent for the fact that when God sends cataclysmic judgment, He rescues both believers and their children but allows unbelievers and their children to face judgment. I believe that during the Tribulation the young children of unbelievers will have the opportunity to believe in Christ as they come of age. Those who die during the Tribulation before they are old enough to understand the claims of the gospel will be taken to heaven to be with Christ. Finally, regardless of which view one holds, the one fact we can all rest in is that God is a God of love, compassion, mercy, and justice. Whatever He does when the Rapture occurs will be wise, righteous, and fair. God loves our children more than we do. Indeed, they are "precious in His sight."

6. Patrick Johnstone and Jason Mandryk, *Operation World,* rev. ed., (Tyrone, Georgia: Authentic Media), 2001.

7. Tim LaHaye and Ed Hindson, *Global Warning: Are We on the Brink of WWIII?* (Eugene, OR: Harvest House, 2007), 169.

8. Charles Dyer, *Rise of Babylon: Sign of the End Times,* (Wheaton, IL: Tyndale, 1991), 168.

Chapter 9

1. Tim LaHaye and Ed Hindson, *Global Warning: Are We on the Brink of WWIII?* (Eugene, OR: Harvest House, 2007), 169.

2. John Walvoord, *The Nations in Prophecy,* (Grand Rapids, MI: Zondervan, 1967), 173.

3. Charles C. Ryrie, *The Best Is Yet to Come,* (Chicago: Moody, 1981), 110–11. This same view is supported by many others. See Ed Hindson, *Is the Antichrist Alive and Well?* (Eugene, OR: Harvest House, 1998),

127–28; Arno Froese, "United Europe's Power Play," in *Foreshocks of Antichrist,* ed. William T. James (Eugene, OR: Harvest House, 1997), 284–87.

4. Thomas Ice and Timothy Demy, *The Truth About America in the Last Days* (Eugene, OR: Harvest House, 1998), 21.

5. Ed Dobson, *The End* (Grand Rapids, MI: Zondervan, 1997), 167.

Chapter 10

1. Charles C. Ryrie, *The Best Is Yet to Come,* (Chicago: Moody, 1981), 111.

2. John Bolton, *Surrender Is Not an Option* (New York: Threshold Editions, 2007), 371. Bolton was the former U.S. ambassador to the United Nations under President George W. Bush.

3. Etgar Lefkovitz, "U.S. Christians 'morally' support Israel," *Jerusalem Post,* April 10, 2008, http://joshuafund.blogspot.com/. The poll was conducted by the Joshua Fund.

4. David R. Francis, "Economist Tallies Swelling Cost of Israel to U.S.," *Christian Science Monitor,* December 9, 2002, www.csmonitor.com/2002/1209/p16s01-wmgn.htm.

5. Yitzhak Ben Horin, "Israel Still Top Recipient of U.S. Foreign Aid," Ynetnews .com, Feb 8, 2007.

6. Michael J. Vlach, "The Church as a Replacement of Israel: An Analysis of Supersessionism," (PhD diss., Southeastern Baptist Theological Seminary, 2004), xv.

7. "The term 'replacement theology' (cf. 'Christian supersessionism') is a relatively new term in Christian theology," says Ronald E. Diprose, *Israel in the Development of Christian Thought* (Rome: Instituto Biblico Evangelico Italiano, 2000), 31, n. 2.

8. Vlach, "The Church as a Replacement of Israel," 10.

9. Diprose, *Israel in the Development of Christian Thought,* 31. Vlach, in his PhD dissertation on the subject, describes both the method of replacement

theology and the theology or outcome it produces: "In the realm of hermeneutics, supersessionists argue that: (1) the New Testament has interpretive priority over the Old Testament; (2) national Israel functioned as a type of the New Testament church; and (3) the New Testament indicates that Old Testament prophecies regarding national Israel are being fulfilled with the church" (Vlach, "The Church as a Replacement of Israel," xvii).

10. Arnold G. Fruchtenbaum, *Israelology: The Missing Link in Systematic Theology*, rev. ed. (Tustin, CA: Ariel Ministries, 1994) is an expanded version of his PhD dissertation at New York University.

11. This study is provided in Fruchtenbaum, *Israelology*, 684–99.

12. Fruchtenbaum, *Israelology*, 699 (emphasis original). See also Barry E. Horner, *Future Israel: Why Christian Anti-Judaism Must Be Challenged*, NAC Studies in Bible and Theology, ed. E. Ray Clendenen (Nashville: B&H Academic, 2007), 228; and E. D. Burton, *Galatians* (Edinburgh: T&T Clark, 1968), 358.

13. Robert L. Thomas, *Revelation 1–7: An Exegetical Commentary*, (Chicago: Moody, 1992), 476.

14. Passages include: Genesis 12:7; 13:14–15; 15:18; 17:8; Leviticus 26:33, 43; Deuteronomy 26:9; 30:1–11; Joshua 24:20–28; 2 Samuel 7:11–16; Ezra 4:1–3; Psalm 102:13–20; Isaiah 11:11–12; 18:7; 27:12–13; 29:1, 8; 44; 60:8–21; 66:18–22; Jeremiah 3:17–18; 7:7; 11:10–11; 23:3–6; 25:5; 29:14; 30:7, 10; 31:2, 10, 23, 31–34; 33:4–16; 50:19; Ezekiel 11:17; 20:33–37; 22:19–22; 28:25; 36:23–24, 38; 37:21–22; 39:28; Daniel 12:1; Hosea 3:4–5; Joel 3:20–21; Amos 9:9, 14–15; Micah 2:12; 3:9–10; 4:7, 11–12; Zephaniah 2:1–3; Zechariah 7:7–8; 8:1–8; 10:6–12; 12:2–10; 13:8–9; 14:1, 5, 9; Malachi 3:6.

15. Relevant passages include: Matthew 19:28; 23:37; Luke 21:24, 29–33; Acts 15:14–17; Romans 11; Revelation 11:1–2; 12.

16. For an excellent presentation of the dangers of replacement theology and a defense of Israel's right to the land, see Horner, *Future Israel.*

17. Note the following references in Genesis: 12:1–3, 7–9; 13:14–18; 15:1–18; 17:1–27; 22:15–19; 26:2–6, 24–25; 27:28–29, 38–40; 28:1–4, 10–22; 31:3, 11–13; 32:22–32; 35:9–15; 48:3–4, 10–20; 49:1–28; 50:23–25

18. Charles H. Dyer, *The Rise of Babylon: Sign of the End Times* (Wheaton, IL: Tyndale, 1991), 170.

19. Ryrie, *Best Is Yet to Come,* 112.

20. Ryrie, *Best Is Yet to Come,* 112.

Appendix A

1. Charles H. Dyer, *World News and Bible Prophecy* (Wheaton, IL: Tyndale, 1995), 214.

2. "The Pledge of Allegiance to the United States Flag," www.homeofheroes .com/hallofheroes/1st_floor/flag/1bfc_pledge.html.

3. This story was taken from Steven J. Lawson, *Heaven Help Us* (Colorado Springs: NavPress, 1995), 99–100.

Appendix B

1. Both of these excerpts are used with permission. Quotes in these excerpts are taken from the New International Version (NIV).

ARE WE HEADED FOR A
NUCLEAR JIHAD?

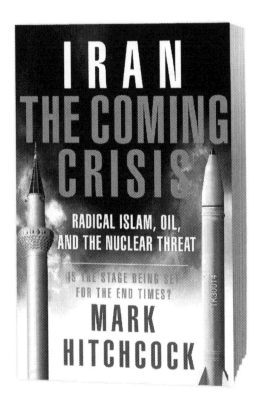

In a prophecy written over 2,500 years ago, Ezekiel 38–39 foretells Iran's future. Iran, Russia, and other Islamic nations will invade Israel in the end times. Today, the connection between Iran and Russia grows stronger. How close is this invasion?

ANSWERS TO YOUR END TIMES QUESTIONS

Prophecy expert Mark Hitchcock invites you to take an in-depth look at the end times and provides a positive word of hope for your family in a time when world events are in upheaval.

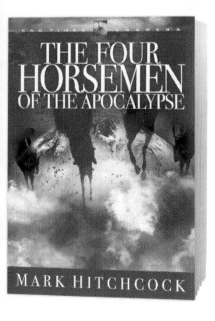

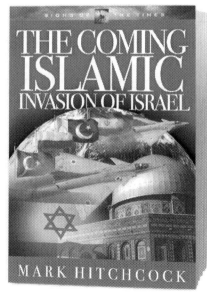

Printed in the United States
by Baker & Taylor Publisher Services